Expect the Best,
[signature]

DISTINCTIVE HOMES OF America

VOLUME IV
LAKE GENEVA
WISCONSIN

BY GLENN D. HETTINGER, AIA, ICAA

CREDITS

PUBLISHED BY

GDH Architects, P.A.

dba DISTINCTIVE HOMES OF AMERICA

38 Valencia Street, Suite 200
Ponte Vedra Beach, FL 32082
904.881.8100

www.DistinctiveHomesOfAmerica.com

GLENN D. HETTINGER, AIA, ICAA

Principal Photographer, Author and Managing Editor.
Concept & Project Direction

18 CONTRIBUTING PHOTOGRAPHERS

Matt Mason Photography, John Faier Photography, Michael Abraham, Jason Bernard,
John Engerman, Paul Schlissman, Kolbe Windows, Parisi Photography and Studio 3 Productions.

Carol Lavin Bernick, Linda Oyama Bryan, Ken Dahlin, Tom Keefe, Ron McCormack,
Bill Meyer Photography, Mike Pfammatter, Bruce Thompson, Bob Webster.

CONTRIBUTING WRITERS

Many Homeowners, Architects, Interior Designers and General Contractors of the
56 featured homes gave insight into the distinctiveness of their design and building projects.
They are quoted in the home layouts in and around the pictures of their impressive work.

Copyright © 2013 Glenn D. Hettinger
Produced and published by Glenn D. Hettinger, AIA, ICAA
All rights reserved. No portion of this book may be reproduced – mechanically, electronically,
or by any other means including photocopying – without written permission from the publisher,
except for brief passages that may be quoted for reviews.

Library of Congress Control Number: 00000000000.
First Edition

ISBN-13: 978-0-615-76101-5
ISBN-10: 0615761011

Printed in Dongguan, China by Crash Paper
First Printing: May 2013
10 9 8 7 6 5 4 3 2 1

JACKET/ COVER DESIGN: The seven homes featured span the diverse spectrum of
architectural design that makes Lake Geneva a one-of-a-kind community, and represents
the unique people that make it their home.

228 pages, with more than 700 full-color pictures.

visit **www.DistinctiveHomesOfAmerica.com** for further information.

ENDORSEMENT

"Once again, Glenn Hettinger seeks out and describes
truly distinctive homes in unique communities across America.
Lavishly illustrated and fluently written, he sets the bar high
for those who would otherwise dot our landscapes
with uninspired homes. Every homeowner, contractor, or architect
should have all his books in their library
and look twice before they build."

Jeremiah Eck, FAIA
Author of *'The Distinctive Home,'*
'The Face of Home,' and most recently, *'House in the Landscape*;'
Partner, Eck I MacNeely Architects, inc. - Boston, MA;
former lecturer at Harvard University's
Graduate School of Design

© Glenn Hettinger

ACKNOWLEDGMENTS

"IF YOU'RE LUCKY ENOUGH TO LIVE AT THE LAKE YOU'RE LUCKY ENOUGH"

Anyone who has lived or vacationed around Geneva Lake has been blessed. That is why I hope that what is shared in this book will be a blessing to all who read it. I have to first thank all of the homeowners who graciously shared their distinctive homes in this way. I had to take these pictures when the sun and clouds were just right and usually on short notice. I so appreciate the cooperation and hospitality that the homeowners have granted me.

Special recognition goes to all of the architects, home designers, interior designers, builders, Realtors and other professionals for their distinctive creations. And, I seek their forgiveness for hounding them for quotes, photographs and other information about the homes on which they worked. It is my hope that all will benefit from this additional exposure of their outstanding creations.

Thanks go to the many contributing photographers, both amateur and professional. The book is so much better due to their contributions. I must especially single out the fabulous photographs from Matt Mason Photography, John Faier Photography, Michael Abraham, Jason Bernard, John Engerman, Paul Schlissman, Parisi Photography, Studio 3 Productions and Kolbe Windows.

My great appreciation goes to my brother-in-law and sister-in-law Jim & Jane Pickle. They have hosted my family with joyful hospitality for decades at their Abbey Resort condominium. Jim's endearing enthusiasm for taking me on countless boat rides made this book possible. It enabled me to take my pictures from the lake and for my countless photo walks over the entire footpath.

"O Captain! My Captain!"

Most of all, I am so blessed to have the support of my wonderful wife Jean, our four fantastic sons Sam, Ben, Greg & Alex, and four fabulous daughters-in-law Laura, Jenny, Heather and Kira. They have all tolerated my enthusiastic taking of pictures of architecture wherever we travel together. This book fulfills another bucket list item for me, but it is dedicated to my family as a big thank you for their continued love and support.

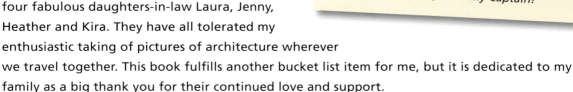

DISTINCTIVE HOMES OF America©

GENEVA LAKE
WALWORTH COUNTY
5,262 ACRES | 2013

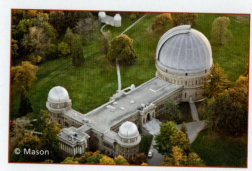
Yerkes Observatory, established in 1897.

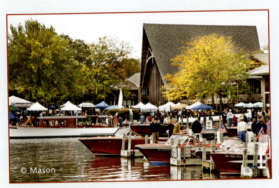
Antique & Classic Boat Show

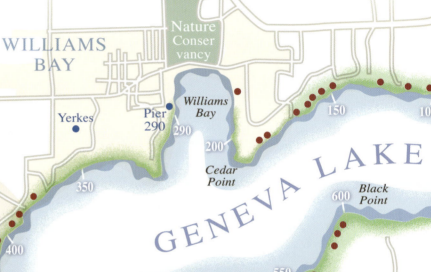

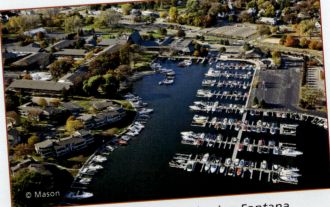
The Abbey Resort, anchoring Fontana for over 50 years. www.TheAbbeyResort.com

PRODUCED BY
© **Distinctive Homes** *of America*

Lake Geneva, Wisconsin

This tabletop book presents over 700 colored pictures of 56 *Distinctive Homes of America,* all located on the shores of Geneva Lake. Some homes are so well designed and built that they are without peer. Each home has special features that set it apart in a positive way.

Our goal was to present the 56 homes and surrounding communities in the best possible light. Twenty different photographers contributed their best photography to accomplish this. The principle photography was shot by Glenn Hettinger as he walked the 21-mile footpath circling the entire waterfront many times. He also took waterfront pictures of most of the homes from his brother-in-law's boat.

The featured homes are arranged in the book by their pier numbers. It begins with pier 21 on the northeast shore and runs counter clockwise to pier 888 on the southeast shore. Please enjoy your tour of these homes, many of which that have never been previously photographed.

Location

Geneva Lake is the correct name for the lake and the town on the east end is Lake Geneva. But most everyone refers to the whole area as Lake Geneva.

The Potawatomi Indians called the lake "Kishwauketo" meaning "clear water" or "sparkling water." In 1835 John Brink a frontier surveyor came to the lake and named the Wisconsin lake "Geneva" after his home in Geneva, NY. He also noted the location of the town site which later became the city of Lake Geneva.

Now its well-deserved reputation for pristine, clear, spring-fed water attracts boat lovers from all over the world.

It is located in the state's southeastern corner in the center of a triangle formed by Milwaukee, Chicago and Madison. Little wonder that the lake's luxury, serenity and fun attract over a million visitors annually.

WISCONSIN

EXPERIENCING THE WATERS *of Geneva Lake*

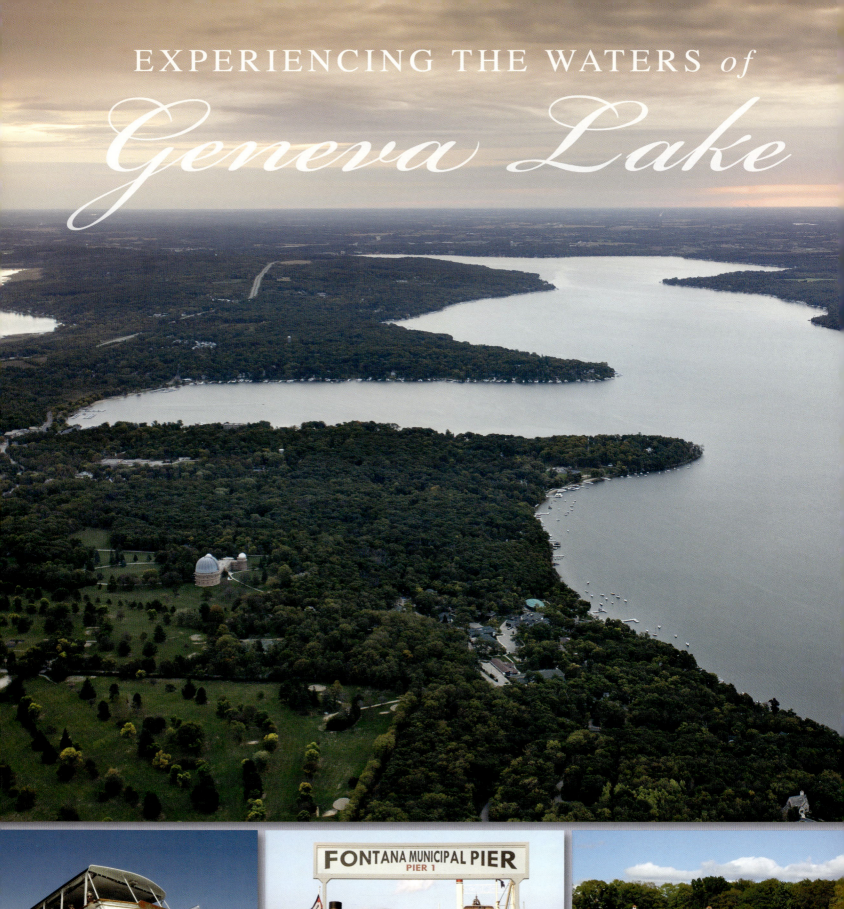

THE TRADITIONS OF
Lake Living

Gage Marine, "stewards of history," carry on the traditions of lake living. Company roots trace back to the excursion boat business in 1873 with the launching of the original Lady of the Lake. It has since evolved into a number of businesses that serve both visitors and lakefront owners, all while enhancing the lake experience.

Lake Geneva Cruise Line operates a collection of eight vintage yachts. Their fleet is the only one of its' type in North America. Leaving the dock, passengers are transported away from any stress to enjoy the tranquil lake beauty. Life slows to the speed of a gentle steamer from an era gone by. As the scenery unfolds, passengers relax and have time to appreciate each other and the allure of the lake. Daily tours vary from the iconic Mail Boat to full meal cruises. Private parties can be hosted from early spring thru late fall.

The Gage Marine sales and service business has been serving customers for generations and provides some of the finest boat repair and boat sales choices in the region.

The Antique & Wood Boat Center features a small museum space and workshop where guests can observe craftsmen perform repairs on the large excursion steamers and vintage mahogany boats.

"Gage-Hacker" custom wood boats were created in the 1950's after they hired famed naval architect John Hacker to design the beautiful and smooth riding boats. And they are building beautiful boats again.

Gage Marina in Williams Bay is a multifaceted, lakeside destination featuring a marina, restaurant, showroom and wood boat center. There you can enjoy lake living even if you don't live on the lake. The marina campus is living history being rebuilt with salvaged materials from over 100 local structures and boats. Pier 290 restaurant features casual dining, outdoor decks, white sand beach, outdoor bar, fire pits and private dining lounge.

CONTENTS

PAGE		DESCRIPTION			
14		"What Makes a Home Distinctive?"			
16	HOME 1	**PIER 21**	1937 & 2012	Eclectic	*"The R. Harold Zook Coach House"*
20	HOME 2	**PIER 48**	1984	English Country Manor	*"Hillcroft"*
24	HOME 3	**PIER 50**	2008	Newport Shingle Style	*"Summerwood"*
28	HOME 4	**PIER 62**	1905 & 1998	Georgian Revival	*"The Driehause Estate"*
34	HOME 5	**PIER 74**	2008	English Tudor Revival	*"Stoney Hollow"*
38	HOME 6	**PIER 74B**	1996	Rustic Chalet / Lodge	*"Forrest Edge"*
40	HOME 7	**PIER 90**	2011	Old French Manor	*"Chez Mere"*
46	HOME 8	**PIER 97**	2009	Rustic Prairie Lodge	
48	HOME 9	**PIER 101**	2008	Victorian Shingle Style	
52	HOME 10	**PIER 116**	1892, 1955 & 2012	Classic Victorian	*"Victorian Lady"*
55	HOME 11	**PIER 132A**	1960, 1990 & 2007	Classic American	*"Jerseyhurst"*
60	HOME 12	**PIER 156**	2005	Arts & Crafts / Shingle Style Cottage	*"Chateau North"*
62	HOME 13	**PIER 161**	2012	Dutch Colonial	*"The Eddins Home"*
66	HOME 14	**PIER 163**	1993	Wrightian International Modernism	*"The Koranda Home"*
70	HOME 15	**PIER 163A**	2012	Stone English Manor Revival	*"The Kallergis Home"*
72	HOME 16	**PIER 166**	1998	French Country	*"The Lundstrom Home"*
74	HOME 17	**PIER 182**	2011	English Tudor Revival	*"Parkhaven"*
78	HOME 18	**PIER 183**	1998	French Estate Home	
82	HOME 19	**PIER 233**	2004	Cape Cod Cottage	*"The Nicolosi Home"*
84	HOME 20	**PIER 363**	2010	Hampton Shingle Style	*"Angle's Flight"*
88	HOME 21	**PIER 378**	2005	Shingle Style Estate	*"Summer Wind"*
90	HOME 22	**PIER 394A**	2011	Shingle Style Estate	*"Camp Lake Geneva"*
96	HOME 23	**PIER 397**	1912 & 2001	Prarie Style	*"Deepwood"*
98	HOME 24	**PIER 457**	1890 & 2000	Greek Revival	*"The Pillars"*
100	HOME 25	**PIER 493**	2000	Shingle Style Estate	*"The Shodeen Home"*
104	HOME 26	**PIER 495**	1980 & 1999	Contemporary Oriental Cottage	*"Casa ve Ventanas"*
108	HOME 27	**PIER 501**	2011	Modern Shingle Style	*"Bluebird Day"*
112	HOME 28	**PIER 502A**	2011	Nantucket Shingle Style	*"Westgate"*
116	HOME 29	**PIER 502B**	2010	Shingle Style	*"Westgate"*

© Matt Mason

CONTENTS

PAGE	DESCRIPTION			
118	HOME 30	**PIER 505**	1977 & 2007 — Contemporary	
122	HOME 31	**PIER 507**	2007 & 2011 — Shingle Style – *"Evergreen"*	
126	HOME 32	**PIER 510**	2000 — Contemporary Shingle Style – *"The Morris Family Home"*	
130	HOME 33	**PIER 518**	1918 & 2006 — Eclectic Craftsman Lodge & Adirondack – *"Clear Sky Lodge"*	
134	HOME 34	**PIER 548**	2010 — English Country Revival – *"Le Manoir"*	
136	HOME 35	**PIER 548**	2010 — English Country Revival – *"La Maison du Lac"*	
138	HOME 36	**PIER 548**	2002 — French Chateau – *"Chateau de Vie"*	
140	HOME 37	**PIER 549**	2000 — French Provincial – *"Chateau Du Lac"*	
144	HOME 38	**PIER 553**	2011 — Contemporary American Farmhouse	
146	HOME 39	**PIER 555**	2000 — Lake Cottage Shingle Style – *"The Braley Home"*	
150	HOME 40	**PIER 558**	2001 — Lake Shingle Style – *"Gudvalsignat Hem"*	
155	HOME 41	**PIER 574**	2001 & 2011 — Colonial Revival – *"Stones Throw"*	
158	HOME 42	**PIER 578**	2000 — Contemporary	
161	HOME 43	**PIER 580**	1888 & 1940's — Queen-Anne Style – *"Black Point Estate"*	
164	HOME 44	**PIER 696**	2006 — Cottage Shingle – *"The Laughridge Home"*	
166	HOME 45	**PIER 700A**	2008 — French Lakefront Manor – *"Welcome Home"*	
170	HOME 46	**PIER 700B**	2005 — Modern Glass Pavilion – *"Windows On Nature"*	
174	HOME 47	**PIER 763**	2011 — Nantucket Shingle Style – *"Timless"*	
178	HOME 48	**PIER 770A**	2007 — Arts & Crafts – *"Ashling"*	
182	HOME 49	**PIER 774B**	1999 — Log Cabin Lodge – *"Whispering Oaks Lodge"*	
186	HOME 50	**PIER 775**	2011 — Shingle Style Estate – *"Irish Oaks"*	
192	HOME 51	**PIER 776**	2010 — Arts & Crafts – *"The Miller Faimly Home"*	
194	HOME 52	**PIER 855**	2003 — Shingle Style Cottage – *"Greenridge"*	
196	HOME 53	**PIER 880**	1901 — Italian Renaissance – *"Stone Manor"*	
198	HOME 54	**PIER 882**	1997 & 2000 — Georgian Revival – *"Expect A Miracle"*	
202	HOME 55	**PIER 887**	1883 & 2009 — Neoclassical – *"Oak Lodge"*	
206	HOME 56	**PIER 888**	2007 & 2011 — Wrightian Usonian Style – *"Arrowhead"*	
218	THIRTY-NINE MORE HOMES of DISTINCTION			
224	DISTINCTIVE GUIDE			

© Glenn Hettinger

WHAT MAKES A HOME
DISTINCTIVE?

Glenn Hettinger enjoying Geneva Lake

What does Webster's Dictionary say?
DISTINCTIVE: *adj.*
Serving to distinguish or set apart from others.
DISTINCT: *adj.*
1. Distinguishable from all others.
2. Easily perceived; clear.
3. Clearly defined; unquestionable.

What does the author say?
Distinctive is used here to indicate homes with unique character, typically designed by an architect as one-of-a-kind. If you invested weeks of walking and boating around Lake Geneva most of these homes would stand out as being different in a positive way. A few are included more for their uniqueness, but most are award-winning designs, spectacular, and/ or grand. Together they provide a plethora of home design ideas and details worth imitating.

How were the 56 Distinctive Homes of America, Volume IV — Lake Geneva, WI chosen?
The number one common thread is that all 56 homes look great and look like they were designed by a talented architect. All 56 homes are tastefully designed with sensitivity to their client's program, site constraints, timing, budget, and attention to proportions and details.

Other considerations included: Were they considered the most beautiful homes? ...the best designed homes? ...the best representative of a certain architectural style? ...the most unique homes? ...or the homes with the most unusual history?

How was Lake Geneva, WI chosen for this type of book?
It is a beautiful community that has a wide variety of distinctive homes. The shores of Geneva Lake have an attractive mix of Cottage/Shingle, Arts & Crafts, Prairie Style and Classic Revival styles. Home sizes vary from large estates to small cottages. Home sites range from very steep hillsides to flat sites. And home ages stretch over 125 years. In short, it is rich with photogenic subjects for this type of book.

Why are there 56 featured homes in the book?
While Lake Geneva, WI is rich with hundreds of "Distinctive Homes," the author chose to limit this book to 56 homes to allow enough pages to present each home. By one perspective, 56 homes give the reader a lot to look at. But, by another perspective only 56 homes out of thousands of homes in a prestigious community is exclusive company.

Why were some other homes not included?
Some other homes may have appeared in this book if: 1) the author had discovered them; 2) the view angles for quality photographs were more accessible; 3) the home had been completed and ready to be photographed by November, 2012; or 4) the home owners had agreed to have their home included.

How were the 700 photographs obtained?
The goal was to use the best images available. The author took about 575 of the photographs and the other 125 were contributed from 18 other professional and amateur photographers. All of these additional pictures were very welcomed and the contributing photographers are credited several places. Any photos taken on private property were done with permission from the homeowners.

DISTINCTIVE HOME I

THE R. HAROLD ZOOK COACH HOUSE

The Architect – "This home is distinct due to the unique scale of spaces that blend a robust palette of materials and the complementary details – both of which tell the story about the home's origins and how it has evolved. Our challenge was to address the client's programmatic requirements of converting a weekend getaway into a full-year residence. We had to add extensive modernization of the home's various systems, while respecting and enhancing the rich architecture of Harold Zook's original design. The home marries a range of architectural languages from which we derived inspiration and expanded upon throughout the home."

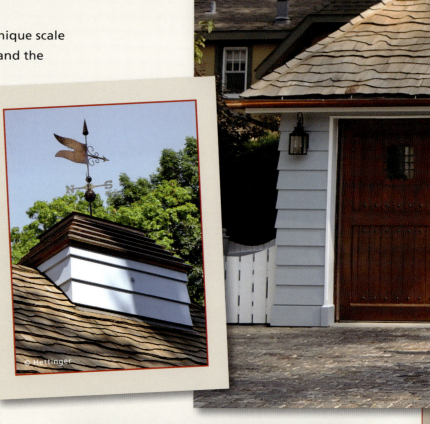

DESCRIPTION / RESOURCES		
BUILT	1937; Remodel 2012	
TOTAL AREA	2,100 SF on 2 Levels	
STYLE	Eclectic	
ARCHITECTS	1937 - The late R.H. Zook - Chicago, IL (1889 - 1940) 2012 - MGLM Architects - Chicago, IL - Peter LoGiudice	
INTERIOR DESIGN	2012 - MGLM Architects - Chicago, IL - Peter LoGiudice	
G.C.	Lowell Mgt. Services - Lake Geneva, WI - Scott Lowell	
LANDSCAPE DESIGN	Mariani Landscape - Lake Bluff, IL	
HARDSCAPE	Masonry by Fernando - Lake Bluff, IL	
PHOTOGRAPHY	Bill Meyer Photography & Glenn Hettinger, AIA	

above: One of Zook's interior trademarks was to graduate the height of the horizontal wood finish from tallest at the bottom to shortest at the top.

far right: Another Zook trademark was to incorporate 'his spider web pattern' at multiple 'memory points,' like the stair railing and the fireplace screen, designed by MGLM Architects.

above: We begin our 21-mile tour around the lake on the foot path in front of pier 21. Here it is manicured while at a few other places it is downright treacherous.

48

DISTINCTIVE HOME II

"Hillcroft"

THE O'NEILL FAMILY HOME

The Owners – "We love the way that our home was designed and built to hug the natural terrain and to become a part of it."

The Interior Designers – "We always strive to create an interior that is both appropriate to the architecture of the residence and the lifestyle of the owner. In this case, the O'Neill's had a large collection of clippings that had been accumulated in anticipation of building this wonderful family home. With a good deal of editing, the warm and elegant interior that you see was created. Some of the rugs were purchased in London and the antiques were found both here and abroad. A well-done interior has staying power and the O'Neill residence proves it. Very little has changed since the home and its interiors were completed, in 1984."

DESCRIPTION / RESOURCES		
BUILT	1984	
TOTAL AREA	18,000 SF on 3 Levels	
STYLE	English Country Manor	
ARCHITECT	Fred Polito Architect - Northbrook, IL	
INTERIOR DESIGN	Interiors II, Ltd. - Chicago, IL - Barbara Lioni & James Zidlicky	
G.C.	Scherrer Construction Co. Inc. - Burlington, WI - Jim Scherrer	
KITCHEN	Wisconsin Cabinets	
PHOTOGRAPHY	Glenn Hettinger, AIA	

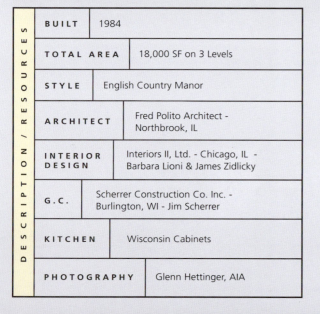

DISTINCTIVE HOME III

"Summerwood"

Architect – "Known as '*The Poolhouse*,' this east coast shingle style building was designed as an 'accessory' lakeside structure for the Owner's multi-acre family compound. Despite having a full kitchen and four guest bedrooms and baths, it's primary function is for family gatherings and entertaining at the lakeshore and pool. The generous wrap-around porch includes a large portion in the center that can be screened at the push of a button with Phantom Screens, enclosing the bbq and outdoor dining areas when needed. The green-stained cedar shingle roof speaks to the original Green Gables Estate built on the property by William Wrigley, Jr."

DESCRIPTION / RESOURCES	BUILT	2008
	TOTAL AREA	Unlisted SF on 2 Levels
	STYLE	Newport Shingle Style
	HOME DESIGN	McCormack + Etten /Architects - Lake Geneva, WI
	INTERIOR DESIGN	Page One Interiors - Adele Lampert - Barrington, IL
	G.C.	Scherrer Construction Co., Inc. - Jim Scherrer - Burlington, WI
	WINDOWS	Marvin Windows
	ZINK ROOFING	Tuschall Engineering
	DOCKS	Gage Marine Services - Williams Bay, WI
	PHOTOGRAPHY	Adele Lampert & Glenn Hettinger, AIA

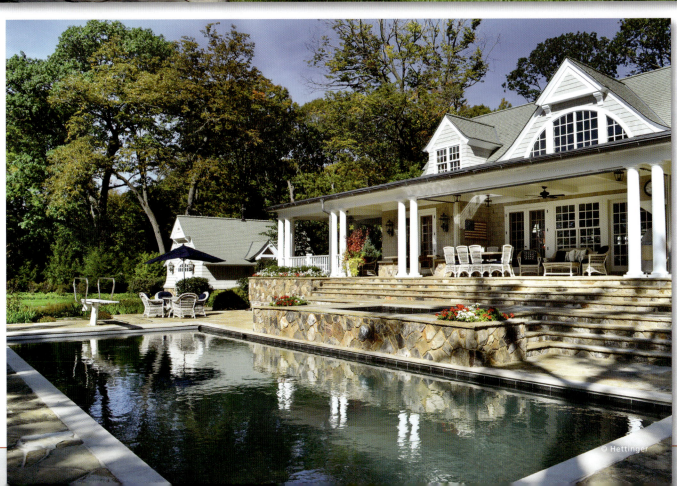

right: A small portion of the 21-Mile Shore Path that is in front of this home. This unique footpath is a public right-of-way that takes on many different looks as it circles the entire lake. Note that some publications list the total shoreline distance as 26 miles?

above: The U.S. Mailboat Tour – As seen on the Travel Channel, CBS News and the Today Show; this is the only maritime mail delivery of its type in the country. The mailmen leaps onto the pier, places the mail in the box and jumps back aboard - while the boat never stops.

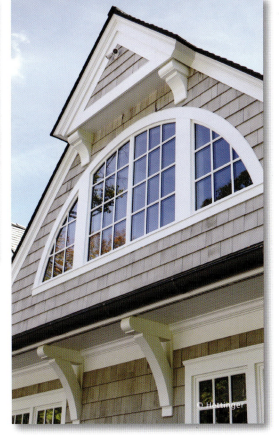

The Owner – "Good design pays over time. The building was correctly situated on the plot, far enough back from the lake and positioned to capture the spring winds."

DISTINCTIVE HOME IV

"The Driehaus Estate"

History – This beautifully restored Georgian Revival home was built in 1905 by Norman W. Harris, founder of Harris Bank in Chicago. It was originally known as Wadsworth Hall, in honor of Mr. Harris' mother, a cousin of Henry Wadsworth Longfellow. The famed Olmstead Brothers created a landscape filled with meandering paths, private gardens and multiple teahouses. In 1998 the 36-acre property was acquired by Chicago businessman and philanthropist Richard H. Driehaus. It is now known as Glanworth Gardens to honor the ancestral home of his mother in County Cork, Ireland.

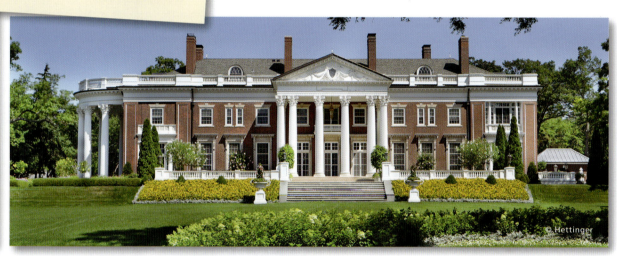

"When I first entered the house, I was overwhelmed by the magnificence of the Great Hall, the Library's cross-sawn oak detailing and the Dining Room's ornamental plaster."

BUILT	1905; Restoration 1999	
TOTAL AREA	22,600 SF on 3 Levels	
STYLE	Georgian Revival	
HOME DESIGN	1999: Harley Ellis Devereaux - Chicago, IL *Original:* Shelpley, Rutan & Coolidge - Boston, MA	
INTERIOR DESIGN	The Gettys Group - Chicago, IL - Andrew Fay	
G.C.	1999: Gilbank Construction, Inc. - Clinton, WI	
LANDSCAPE DESIGN	1999: Louis Wasserman & Associates; Terry Guen Design Associates; *Original:* Olmstead Brothers - Boston, MA	
WINDOWS	Lake Geneva Window & Door Williams Bay, WI - Kolbe Windows	
PHOTOGRAPHY	John Faier Photography - Chicago, IL Glenn Hettinger, AIA	

© John Faier

"In order to complete everything before the Millennium, there were times we required up to 150 workers and tradesmen, seven days-a-week."

"With my passion for classical architecture and historic preservation, I knew I wanted to restore the home and was ready for a challenge of this magnitude. We respected the architecture, history and surrounding landscape design, identifying reference points to the estate's original plans. At the time, it was the largest project in Lake Geneva."

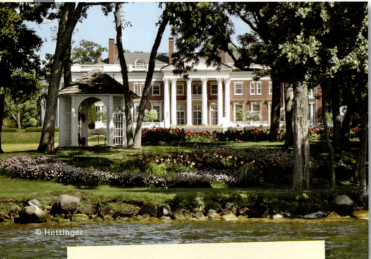

The Interior Designer – "To unify the indoor and outdoor areas, we referred to renowned gardens from around the world as inspiration. Rooms were fully restored to original grandeur and improved with features enhancing the original architecture or supporting modern expectations. The results maintained the ambiance of 1905 yet allowed for 21st century lifestyles."

The Architect – "What a privilege it was to be part of the team restoring this magnificent 14-bedroom mansion. The challenge was to bring the home, which was in a state of decline, into the 21st century while preserving its original elegant design. Restoration experts were consulted extensively."

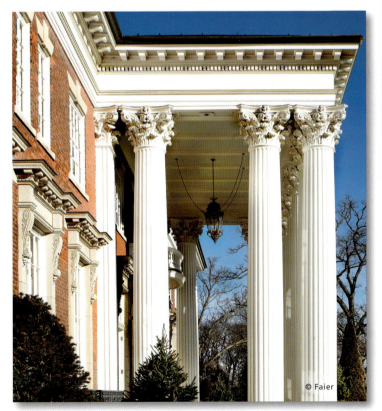

"The east patio was recreated with a swimming pool added to replicate the loggia. Two outdoor porches were enclosed, the forecourt completed and a weathervane added to the carriage house that was part of the original design. Many landscaping features, such as the potager and path by the lake, were reconstructed in the same location as the Olmsted Brothers original master plan."

DISTINCTIVE HOME V

"StoneyHollow"

Built in 2008, it was intentionally built to look decades older. This estate also includes *"The Hollow,"* an award winning entertainment pavilion facing the woods, and a boathouse on the lakeshore near the private boat slips and dock.

Architect –"Inspired by country homes throughout the British Isles, the massive ceiling trusses and soaring wall of 27 leaded glass windows frame the extraordinary views of Geneva Lake. Whether entertaining or having a quiet glass of wine for two, this room is the gathering place at '*StoneyHollow*.'"

"Designed and built in Costa Rica, the antique glass and mahogany windows throughout were transported to the US via banana boat in order to get priority clearance through customs to prevent construction delays *and over-ripe bananas!*"

"A cozy brick-walled dining room looks out on the side garden. The fireplace was inspired by one we found at Villa Feltrinelli in Lake Garda, Italy. Crafted by a local father and son, the fireplace is made of solid English beech."

DESCRIPTION/RESOURCES		
BUILT	2008	
TOTAL AREA	13,000 SF on 3 Levels	
STYLE	English Tudor Revival	
HOME DESIGN	Jason R. Bernard Architects - Lake Geneva, WI	
INTERIOR DESIGN	Owner with Jason Bernard's assistance	
KITCHEN DESIGN	Jackie Naylor Interiors, Inc. - Atlanta, GA	
RECOGNITION	Featured in 'At The Lake' - Summer 2012	
PHOTOGRAPHY	Matt Mason Photography - Parisi Photography - Jason Bernard & Glenn Hettinger, AIA	

© Hettinger

© Parisi

"The fireplace, one of eight in the main house, is hand carved limestone in the European style. The grand staircase is constructed of burr oak trees removed from the site for construction and milled specifically for this purpose."

above: 'The Hollow' entertainment pavillion.

right: The inside of the boat house is surprisingly large and provides great lake views and breezes.

DISTINCTIVE HOME VI

"Forest Edge"

The Owners – "We love our end-to-end lake views from every room and being surrounded by towering Oaks. It gives us a 'Lake Tahoe feel' to the home with post & beam construction, stone, etc. We also like the historical significance of being located on the grounds of the original 'Bonnie Brae Estate.'"

The Architect – "The original owners purchased the property in 1995 when it was occupied by the burned-down remnants of a previous house. With its wonderful location over 60 feet above the water and panoramic views up and down the lake, the site had a lot to offer. We began with the foundation of the previous home, expanded the footprint and designed a home that fulfilled the owners' dream of creating a rustic 'north woods lodge' with cedar shingles, half-log siding and ledge stone veneer."

BUILT	1996	
TOTAL AREA	Unlisted SF on 3 Levels	
STYLE	Rustic Chalet / Lodge	
HOME DESIGN	McCormack + Etten / Architects - Lake Geneva, WI	
INTERIOR DESIGN	Ruth Andreasen - Bonita Springs, FL	
G.C.	Monstma Builders, Inc., Delavan, WI - Ted Montsma, retired	
LANDSCAPE DESIGN	The Brickman Group Ltd., LLC - Long Grove, IL	
RECOGNITION	*"On The Lake"* Magazine - Fall 2010	
PHOTOGRAPHY	Glenn Hettinger, AIA	

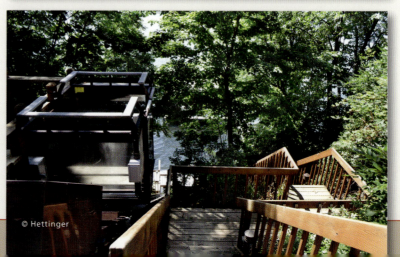

above: The 21-mile foot path sometimes gets very steep as it does in front of this home. But the views make the climbing worthwhile.

left: Some homes like this one are built so high up on the bluffs that the owners install custom elevators to access their lake front amenities.

DISTINCTIVE HOME VII
"Chez Mere"

The Owners – "We tapped our interior designer to serve as the unofficial liaison between the various craftspeople. We've been working with Glen for years; he's a gifted gentleman. Inspired by the view, Lusby blanketed the interiors in a palette of ivories and gray-blues, which repeat throughout the home. The home works because it allows us to have our time together as a family, yet still affords us privacy."

The Architects – "Our challenge was to create a spacious, contemporary retreat that incorporated the charm of the original structure. We wanted the home to feel as if it had been there for a very long time, but thoroughly refitted and modernized."

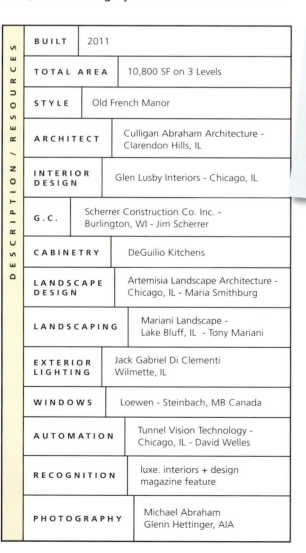

left: The comical and often photographed "All Together Now" (or "The Slick Chicks") sculpted by Guiseppe Palumbo.

DESCRIPTION / RESOURCES		
BUILT	2011	
TOTAL AREA	10,800 SF on 3 Levels	
STYLE	Old French Manor	
ARCHITECT	Culligan Abraham Architecture - Clarendon Hills, IL	
INTERIOR DESIGN	Glen Lusby Interiors - Chicago, IL	
G.C.	Scherrer Construction Co. Inc. - Burlington, WI - Jim Scherrer	
CABINETRY	DeGuilio Kitchens	
LANDSCAPE DESIGN	Artemisia Landscape Architecture - Chicago, IL - Maria Smithburg	
LANDSCAPING	Mariani Landscape - Lake Bluff, IL - Tony Mariani	
EXTERIOR LIGHTING	Jack Gabriel Di Clementi Wilmette, IL	
WINDOWS	Loewen - Steinbach, MB Canada	
AUTOMATION	Tunnel Vision Technology - Chicago, IL - David Welles	
RECOGNITION	luxe. interiors + design magazine feature	
PHOTOGRAPHY	Michael Abraham Glenn Hettinger, AIA	

"We took full advantage of the home's proximity to the lake, which is visible from the major common areas and from the three upstairs suites."

© Abraham

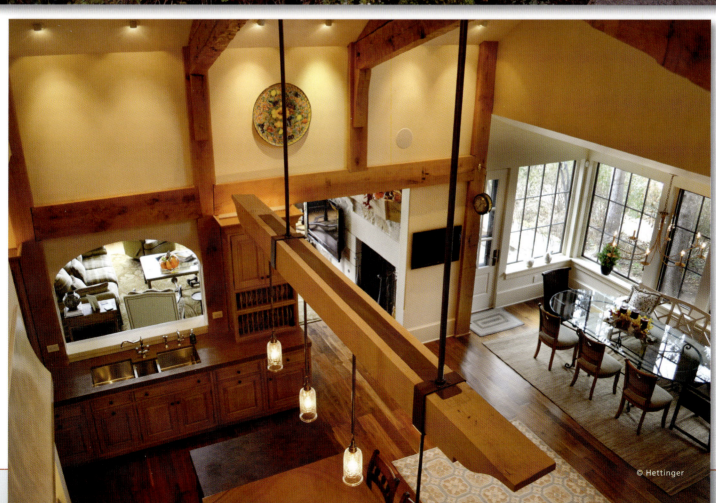
© Hettinger

"In the evening, flickering gas lamps illuminate the grounds, which lend an Old World feel, especially when coupled with the thin layer of stucco that was applied deliberately imperfectly to the stone walls. It looks as if the walls are 200 years old; if we've done our job then the house will get better over time just sitting there. The weather will give it a nice patina."

The Interior Designer – "The major theme is comfort and softness. There's nothing stark about this home, and no hard edges. … We used the same materials, textures and especially colors from the exterior of the home in all the interior design. The goal was to always feel a connection to the outside of the home, no matter where you might be inside."

The Contractor – "In an effort to preserve pine trees on the west and working with less than 10 feet on the east side of the property, this grand home was uniquely built sides first, then center. The center of the lot was kept open as long as possible to allow equipment and materials lakeside."

"Slate roof, stucco siding, specialty masonry and tile, reclaimed timbers, screened porch, and natural gas lanterns lining the driveway added just a few of the many special touches throughout. The adjacent carriage house, 'La Petite Maison,' was built to match the look and feel of the main home."

97

DISTINCTIVE HOME VIII

The Owner / GC – "The home was a labor of love. My wife wanted to create a Colorado rustic yet elegant home that can handle entertaining and family gatherings without being over bearing. Friends often comment that when you enter you feel like you just got a big warm hug."

The Architect – "The architecture required blending the Lake Geneva lifestyle with the Owner's passion for the look and feel of a lodge. A continuous circle of natural materials flows inside and outside, becoming the soul and spirit of a home on the lake."

DESCRIPTION / RESOURCES		
BUILT	2009	
TOTAL AREA	15,000 SF on 3 Levels	
STYLE	Rustic Prarie Lodge	
ARCHITECT	Architectural Environments - St. Charles, IL - Patrick Marzullo	
G.C.	Ciciora Custom Builders, LLC - Mgr John Ciciora; PM Tony Ruggero	
CABINENTRY	Cabaret Cabinetry, Inc - Hayward, WI	
HVAC & PLUM	Expert Pluming & HVAC - Lake Geneva, WI Frank Rizzo & John Stengie	
LANDSCAPING	Botanica Fine Gardens & Landscapes - Lake Geneva, WI	
EXTERIOR LIGHTING	Twilight Solutions - Lake Geneva, WI - Jon Adams	
AUTOMATION	Nugget, Inc. - Barrington, IL	
PHOTOGRAPHY	Glenn Hettinger, AIA	

"Lodge and Prairie Styles are brought together, blending natural materials, stone and cedar, copper and raw steel, seamlessly with the lakefront. And walls of floor to ceiling windows bring in ample natural light."

left: As if the home did not have enough comforts, here's a hammock with a lake view and breeze as well as a TV monitor.

DISTINCTIVE HOME IX

The Owners – "We love the open flowing plan, but it is warm and inviting – reminiscent of an old world lake home for modern day. …The indoor pool is a great feature!"

Architect - "The Owners of this home required special programming for assisted living for a child. They also requested the home be a setting for first class entertainment. The project style was developed from the 'seaside' architecture of the east coast. While many components are 'shingle' vernacular, we put our unique touch to the plans and elevations; exterior 'Grand Porch'

facing the lake, covered porches for three master suites, open floor planning for easy entertainment, many sleeping area's with private baths, lower level amenities for intimate theatre and entertaining and an in-door swimming pool. The 'tower' holds the main level dining for 16 and the upper level is the Owners' private studio. This home offers all the amenities for first class entertainment."

DESCRIPTION / RESOURCES		
BUILT	2008	
TOTAL AREA	9,500 SF on 3 Levels	
STYLE	Victorian Shingle Style	
ARCHITECT	R.R. Browne Architects - West Dundee, IL – Rick Browne	
INTERIOR DESIGN	Ginny Blasco Design Studio, Inc. – Chicago, IL	
CABINETRY	Drury Design: Kitchen & Bath Studio Glen Ellyn, IL – Gail Drury	
LANDSCAPE DESIGN	Botanica Fine Gardens & Landscapes Lake Geneva, WI	
EXTERIOR LIGHTING	Twilight Solutions - Lake Geneva, WI Jon Adams	
POOL CONST.	Anchor Pool & Spa, Huntley, IL - Larry Hayes	
DOCKS	Austin Pier Service, Inc. - Walworth, WI Darrell Frederick	
PHOTOGRAPHY	Glenn Hettinger, AIA	

top: "Our inspiration to create a Master Study on the upper level was twofold: quiet area for work and a fun room to relax and view the water's activity. The small port windows are lowered to accommodate the arm of the telescope. The flooring layout imitates the vaulted pyramidal shape at the ceiling. The study has a half-bath, private wet bar and humidor."

Cabinetry – "Taller cabinets were used to maximize display impact and storage space. Special touches are inset cabinets, a colorful island, black honed tops, white subway tiles, glass knobs and chicken wire to bring a casual elegance with vintage flair."

DISTINCTIVE HOME X

"Victorian Lady"

THE COUFER HOME

The Owners – "We love all parts of our historic home but especially the elongated, curved front porch. It provides us excellent views of beautiful Lake Geneva. And it has been in our family for three generations. So, the mysterious 'C' in the gable naturally stands for Couffer.

This 13-room home was built in 1876 for $8,000. In 1924 it was purchased by the Couffer family. The living room fireplace is made of fieldstone with sculptured granite relief and wood molding above. Natural hand-carved buttonwood wood meanders throughout the home. The windows sparkle with stained, leaded, beveled or unusually high-quality frosted glass panes."

"The *Victorian Lady* is part of the Elgin Club, referring to the town in Illinois where its members resided. It was the first of the camping associations to be established on Geneva Lake and it set the precedent for those that would follow. The club had 20 members, each possessing a lot with fifty-foot of lake frontage."

DESCRIPTION		
BUILT	1892 Remodeled: 1955 + 2012	
TOTAL AREA	2,200 SF on 3 Levels	
STYLE	Classic Victorian	
RECOGNITION	Featured in *Lake Geneva Mag.* - August 1988	
HOME DESIGN	Unknown	
PHOTOGRAPHY	Glenn Hettinger, AIA	

left: Author's award for the "Most Distinctive Weathervane" on the lake.

DISTINCTIVE HOME XI

"Jerseyhurst"
(formerly the Crane Plumbing Estate)

LEE & MARILYN TENZER HOME

The Owners – "We have completed a lot of additions and renovations to our 50-year old home. We love our kitchen, pool house and the special grandchildren bedrooms. The only projects remaining are a tree house and playhouse for the grandchildren."

Interior Designer – "We designed the new very large kitchen and equally large butler's pantry. Hand scraped walnut floors, warm colors of gold, red and green, hand painted tiles and a cozy booth, all welcome guests and family to the kitchen."

"The adjacent butler's pantry/ laundry room/ office was added to support this hub of the house with great cooperation from the Architect, GC and Interior Designer."

DESCRIPTION/RESOURCES		
BUILT	1960 + 1990 & 2007 Additions	
TOTAL AREA	15,000 SF on 4 Levels	
STYLE	Classic American	
ARCHITECT	McCormack + Etten / Architects, LLP Lake Geneva, WI	
INTERIOR DESIGNER	Page One Interiors, Inc. - Barrington, IL - Adele Lampert, ASID	
G.C.	Frank Guido & Engerman Contracting	
KITCHEN	Page One Interiors, Inc.	
RECOGNITION	ASID Kitchen Renovation Award	
PHOTOGRAPHY	Paul Schlismann & Glenn Hettinger, AIA	

"There are other, warm, cozy rooms like the paneled family room with oversized marble fireplace, paneled living room and light breezy porches. The pool house provides yet another atmosphere for summertime fun."

above: The screened porch is certainly a delightful place to be on a beautiful sunny day, but it's an equally great place to read a book while listening to the rain on a rainy day.

left: The monumental stairway provides a lot of 'eye candy' in the entry, but an equal eyeful is your view right through to Geneva Lake.

© Hettinger

© Schlismann

above: Free standing pool house.

below: 'Pantry' for Fiesta Ware collection.

DISTINCTIVE HOME XII
"Chateau North"
THE BAIRD FAMILY HOME

Owners - "Everything about our home was intended to be comfortable for the family and we really relax when we are there. We even have 'napping beds' in our large 32' x 30' family room facing the lake. We also have a pergola off of the kitchen with a retractable roof for outdoor cooking."

Design/ Builder – "We created an expanded version of the Owner's previous lake home on the property.

DESCRIPTION		
BUILT	2005	
TOTAL AREA	5,000 SF on 3 Levels	
STYLE	Arts & Crafts and Shingle Style Cottage	
HOME DESIGN	Engerman Design & Owner Nolan Baird	
INTERIORS	by the Baird Family	
G.C.	Engerman Contracting - Lake Geneva, WI - John Engerman	
WINDOWS	Lake Geneva Window & Door - Williams Bay, WI - Kolbe	
PHOTOGRAPHY	Glenn Hettinger, AIA	

"We built the great room with free spans the width of the House. On the exterior we used flared shingle walls and heavy bracketing which is indicative of the Craftsman Shingle Style era. The upper level lakefront porch embellishes a radius opening reminiscent of the classic sleeping porches found on many lake homes in the old days prior to air conditioning."

DISTINCTIVE HOME XIII

THE EDDINS HOME

The Owners – "We love having lots of light in so many rooms. All of our fabric in our family room is 'Sunbrella' so the kids and dogs can enjoy the furniture without dirtying it, and the sun won't bleach it out."

Architect – "'Instant Classic' had been the response to this new family home built on the north shore of the lake in 2011. Capped by a large fenestrated cupola, the home wraps about a central open stair tower that floods the interior with natural light and draws summer lake breezes through the home, up and out to the exterior again. Every living space enjoys panoramic lake or wooded views. The fact that the interior design was done by the Owners is certainly a testament to their good taste — it's all simply beautiful."

above: 'Sugar' on stairs.

left: 1959 Metropolitan by garage.

BUILT	2012	
TOTAL AREA	4,800 SF on 3 Levels	
STYLE	Dutch Colonial	
ARCHITECTS	McCormack + Etten / Architects - Lake Geneva, WI	
INTERIOR DESIGN	Christie Eddins	
G.C.	South Shore Custom Homes, Inc. - Fontana, WI - Tony Osnacz & Rick Lyman	
KITCHEN DESIGN	Kitchens By Design - Lombard, IL - Vince Baggetto	
LANDSCAPE LIGHTING	Estate Lighting, Inc. - Richmond, IL - Tim Tacheny	
WINDOWS	Kolbe Ultra Sterling Series	
DOCKS	Gage Marine Services - Williams Bay, WI	
PHOTOGRAPHY	Glenn Hettinger, AIA	

above right: The public footpath continues as a gravel path by this home.

right: A fun solution for variable bedding needs at a lake house: a double-decker bunk adds sleepover space to this boy's bedroom.

above: With the bench back pivoting side to side it can be used to eat at the table or to look out to the lake ...an idea borrowed from the Rehoboth Beach, DE boardwalk.

left: The tall and large fenestrated cupola that the architect mentioned.

163

DISTINCTIVE HOME XIV

THE KORANDA HOME

The Owners – "We just love the way this home really does bring the outside in and takes the inside out in a seamless way. It is such a pleasure to live in this special home."

The Architect – "The design of this distinctive home recalls the 'architectural vocabulary' of the iconic International Style house *Fallingwater* by Frank Lloyd Wright. However, this design is a total reinterpretation of the style into a different design responding to the clients' requirements, plan organization and setting."

DESCRIPTION / RESOURCES	BUILT	1993
	TOTAL AREA	6,400 SF on 4 Levels
	STYLE	Wrightian International Modernism
	ARCHITECTURE	Atelier Tilton, LLC - Chicago, IL - John D. Tilton
	INTERIOR DESIGN	Atelier Tilton, LLC - Chicago, IL - John D. Tilton
	G.C.	State Construction Company - Niels Andersen
	STRUCTURE	Cast-in-place concrete with post tensioned concrete cantilevers
	WINDOWS	Hopes Steel Windows & Doors
	MILLWORK	Continental Woodworking
	PHOTOGRAPHY	Glenn Hettinger, AIA Matt Mason Photography

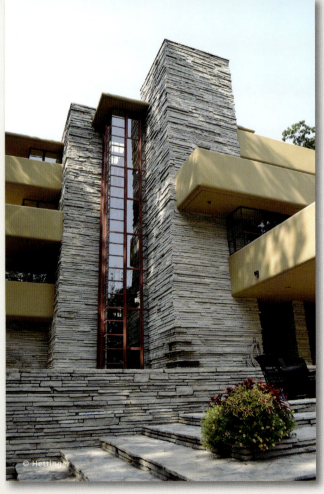

"The 'kit-of-parts' – palette of colors, materials, textures and construction elements are similar – but the composition is totally different."

"The architectural massing of this 4-story home is comprised of a series of stone towers engaged into the unifying concrete floor trays. Each has upturned parapet walls at the cantilevered terraces and balconies. The verticality of the central form spreads out horizontally onto the ground plane, and the stone planters / wing walls radiate out further into the surrounding forested site."

left: "God of Existence" sculpture found in Bhutan market.

DISTINCTIVE HOME XV
THE KALLERGIS HOME

While this home looks like it could be one of the old estate homes, it was actually built brand new in 2012. It has stunning stone and limestone exterior walls, five limestone fireplace chimneys, and a multi-colored slate roof. The large veranda and walkways are thermal blue stone with exterior gaslights. The materials on the new boathouse even match the home.

DESCRIPTION		
	BUILT	2012
	TOTAL AREA	16,000 SF on 4 Levels
	STYLE	Stone English Manor
	ARCHITECT	Culligan Abraham Architecture - Clarendon Hills, IL
	LANDSCAPE DESIGN	ILT Vignocchi Landscape Architects & Contractors - Wauconda, IL
	G.C.	Hummel Construction - Delavan, WI Chris Hummel
	PHOTOGRAPHY	Matt Mason Photography & Glenn Hettinger, AIA

DISTINCTIVE HOME XVI
THE LUNDSTROM HOME

The Owners – "We love the open feeling in our living room, dining room and kitchen area – all with great views of the lake. We also like our stone exterior and the interesting rooflines which create interesting interior ceiling lines."

The Architects - "The soft color palette is articulated with red brick accents and copper roofs. The exterior rubble stone was imported from Oklahoma and painstakingly shaped and parged with mortar to achieve a wonderful old world texture."

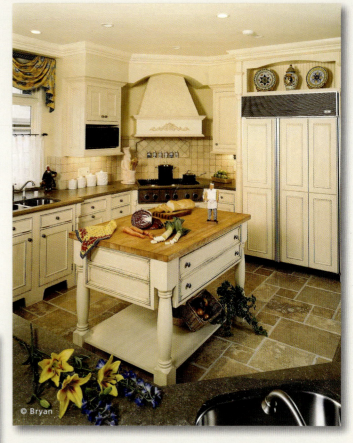

"Steep shake roofs with a soft sweep at the eaves caps the home with a certain charm, appropriate to its French roots."

DESCRIPTION / RESOURCES		
	BUILT	1998
	TOTAL AREA	6,300 SF on 2 Levels
	STYLE	French Country
	HOME DESIGN	McCormack + Etten / Architects - Lake Geneva, WI
	INTERIOR DESIGN	Page One Interiors, Inc - Barrington, IL - Adele Lampert, ASID
	LANDSCAPE DESIGN	Paul Swartz Landscape & Nursery - Burlington, WI
	G.C.	Orren Pickell Building Group, LLC - Northridge, IL
	KITCHEN	Cabinet Works Division of Pickell Building Group
	RECOGNITION	Custom Home mag. Feb. 2001 Excellence in Housing Design - 1999 Gold Key Award Kitchens by Professional Designers Book XIII
	PHOTOGRAPHY	Linda Oyama Bryan & Matt Mason Photography & Glenn Hettinger, AIA

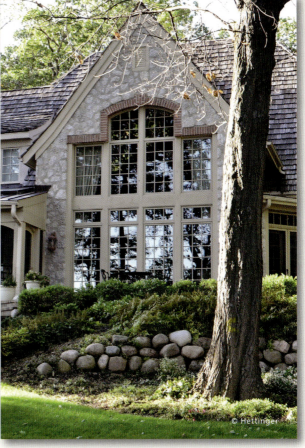

"Despite its considerable size, this home maintains a modest and inviting scale when viewed from either the street or lake approaches."

DISTINCTIVE HOME XVII

"Parkhaven"
THE ZALESKI HOME

The Owners – "We love the stone and reclaimed timbers from mid-west barns that were used on the interior. They give us the classic English Tudor feel that we were seeking. We even built a large and authentic English Pub on the ground floor."

The Architect – "The Owner desired a genuinely old-world character for all materials and finishes used in the home, and the results are simply stunning."

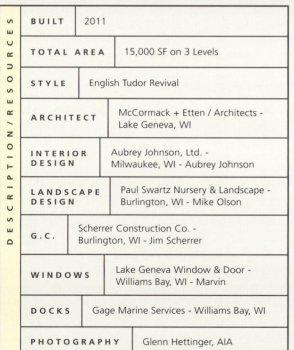

above: The front entry foyer is full of 'eye candy' with amazing interior and exterior vistas in all directions.

DESCRIPTION/RESOURCES		
BUILT	2011	
TOTAL AREA	15,000 SF on 3 Levels	
STYLE	English Tudor Revival	
ARCHITECT	McCormack + Etten / Architects - Lake Geneva, WI	
INTERIOR DESIGN	Aubrey Johnson, Ltd. - Milwaukee, WI - Aubrey Johnson	
LANDSCAPE DESIGN	Paul Swartz Nursery & Landscape - Burlington, WI - Mike Olson	
G.C.	Scherrer Construction Co. - Burlington, WI - Jim Scherrer	
WINDOWS	Lake Geneva Window & Door - Williams Bay, WI - Marvin	
DOCKS	Gage Marine Services - Williams Bay, WI	
PHOTOGRAPHY	Glenn Hettinger, AIA	

"The English Tudor style exterior combines natural stone, timber, and brick herringbone inlay in the timber half-frame gable accents. Those same exterior materials extend into the interior walls and eight fireplaces of this home."

above: Every castle needs a throne.

The GC –"Wisconsin winters were the impetus behind the eight fireplaces and heated floors throughout the home; including the garage, lower level, front porch and 3-season room. This distinctive home's unique features include extensive quarter sawn and hand hewn wood floors, stone accents and hand-forged railings integrated throughout."

DISTINCTIVE HOME XVIII

THE ATHANS HOME

The Owners – "We did want an elegant but comfortable home and that is what we got. It is very well laid out for the flow of people and the use of the rooms."

The Architect – "Timelessness was a goal of the Owner as we started into the design process for this home 20 years ago! The years have passed quickly and this home has well exceeded that time test. It remains one of our most appreciated homes as it graces a wonderful expanse of the Lake Geneva shoreline. Built to last, the palette of exterior materials is simple; slate, stone, copper and iron."

DESCRIPTION/RESOURCES		
BUILT	1998	
TOTAL AREA	7,500 SF on 2 Levels	
STYLE	French Estate Home	
HOME DESIGN	McCormack + Etten / Architects - Lake Geneva, WI	
LANDSCAPE DESIGN	Paul Swartz Landscape & Nursery - Burlington, WI	
WINDOWS	Pella Windows & Doors	
DOCKS	Gage Marine Services - Williams Bay, WI	
PHOTOGRAPHY	Glenn Hettinger, AIA	

"There is a formal elegance and grace to this home rarely seen on the lake, and we are proud to have authored it."

left: The lake path continues in front of the refurbished 'boathouse' which was part of the original Schwinn (bike family) estate.

History – In 1922 Ignatz Schwinn, founder of the world famous bicycle company, built his summer home on this high point overlooking the lake. Members of the Schwinn family owned the estate for four generations up to 1993.

233

DISTINCTIVE HOME XIX

THE NICOLOSI HOME

Architect – "The home was a 'dated,' but well-built ranch style home when purchased by our client. They felt it didn't take advantage of the lake access and views. A variance was required for changes to the home, and a key to that variance approval was that we would 'not overbuild.' The challenge was to create a 'Lake Cottage' style home that met their active lake lifestyle without overbuilding."

"With large dormers and roof pitch increase, we were able to provide additional space while not creating a massive looking home. The screen porch was added giving the details of the home's style while linking the interior to the exterior."

left: Home before 2004 remodel.

BUILT	Remodeled 2004	
TOTAL AREA	3,200 SF on 3 Levels	
STYLE	Cape Cod Cottage	
ARCHITECT	McCormack + Etten / Architects - Lake Geneva, WI	
LANDSCAPE DESIGN	Paul Swartz Landscape & Nursery - Burlington, WI	
G.C.	O'Neil Builders, Inc - Lake Geneva - John O'Neil	
WINDOWS	Marvin Windows	
PIERS/ DOCKS	Austin Pier Service Inc. - Walworth, WI - Darrell Frederick	
PHOTOGRAPHY	Glenn Hettinger, AIA	

"During construction, the owner worked with the G.C. to massage the plan details and finishes while creating the outdoor spaces with Paul Swartz."

DISTINCTIVE HOME XX

"Angel's Flight"

THE KEITH & BETTY GIBSON HOME

The Owners – "For many years we wanted a home that looked like it fit in a lakeside setting. We thought about building a gray shingled home which would sit on a bluff overlooking water. We were finally able to achieve our dream when we found this property. We love our hill and all of our large windows throughout the home that afford us all of those outstanding views of the lake."

Architect – "We tried to include everything on our clients wish list: lots of crown moulding, trim work, stained glass, wraparound porches, domed entry, high beamed ceilings, large chef's kitchen, large library with curved book shelves, secret rooms and the large craft room that she always wanted. The home had to be large but with a cozy warm feeling."

DESCRIPTION / RESOURCES		
BUILT	2010	
TOTAL AREA	11,400 SF on 3 Levels	
STYLE	Hampton Shingle Style	
HOME DESIGN	Cornerstone Designs, Woodinville, WA - Troy Clymes	
INTERIOR DESIGN	Interior Changes, Elkhorn, WI - Beth Welsh	
G.C.	Lowell Management, Lake Geneva, WI - Todd Cauffman	
LANDSCAPE	*Design* - Kelly Designs *Lighting* - Twilight Solutions - Johnathan Adams	
KITCHEN DESIGN	Geneva Cabinet Co. - Peggy Helgeson	
WINDOWS	Lake Geneva Window & Door, Williams Bay, WI - Kolbe Windows	
RECOGNITION	2010 Parade of Homes Better Homes & Gardens Mag. Beautiful Kitchens Mag.	
PHOTOGRAPHY	Kolbe Windows & Glenn Hettinger, AIA	

There was a 100-year old home on the site that gave way to age and termites. It was named *"Angel's Flight"* because there was and still is 100 stairs to climb from the lake to the home. They said that after you walked it you were halfway to heaven – hence the name.

Interior Design – "A cheerful color palette helped bring life and celebration to each room, whether it was brought out in wall colors, in coordinating fabrics, or as treasured artwork hung throughout the home. Working with Betty was like being on a continuous creative hunt which was invigorating and fun. There was no detail too small to leave unconsidered, making this whole house a reflection of welcome and retreat."

© Kolbe

378
DISTINCTIVE HOME XXI
"Summer Wind"

The Owners – "We set out to design and build a warm and welcoming family home befitting this special piece of property with views down the length of Geneva Lake. We worked closely with the architect and builder to create many distinctive personal touches inside and outside to suit our active young family. The result is a home built for living, entertaining and enjoying all that this unique lakeside setting has to offer our family."

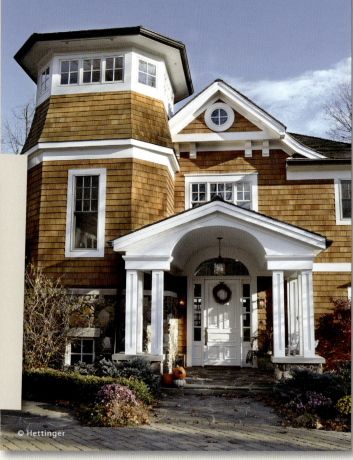

The Architect – "Our client came to us with a beautiful waterfront lot, a love of sailing, and a dream to create a traditional Shingle Style 'Lake Cottage' for their growing family."

DESCRIPTION / RESOURCES		
BUILT	2005	
TOTAL AREA	Unlisted SF on 3 Levels	
STYLE	Shingle Style Estate	
HOME DESIGN	McCormack + Etten / Architects - Lake Geneva, WI	
INTERIOR DESIGN	Page One Interiors, Inc. - Barrington, IL Adele Lampert, ASID & Lakeshore Design - Fontana, WI	
LANDSCAPE DESIGN	Paul Swartz Nursery & Landscape - Burlington, WI	
G.C.	Fisher Fine Home Building, Inc. - Lake Geneva, WI - Tim Fischer	
WINDOWS	VerHalen, Inc. - Brookfield, WI - Pella Architectural Series	
DOCKS	Reed's Construction, LLC - Lake Geneva, WI	
PHOTOGRAPHY	Glenn Hettinger, AIA	

above: The 21-mile footpath continues uninterrupted again.

"Our collaborative design solution was a warm and inviting home that includes formal and informal spaces for the whole family, entertainment spaces, a home office, and a lower level that opens into a sunken outdoor patio. A kitchen island with a teak deck top and other built-ins incorporating teak, mahogany and brass reflect the client's interest in sailing."

394A
DISTINCTIVE HOME XXII
"Camp Lake Geneva"

The Owners – "We wanted a house that blended into the community and took inspiration from the architecture of George Williams College on the lake. The interior is built for comfortable summertime living for both the immediate family as well as larger gatherings."

The Architect – "The dark brown and white color scheme echoes classic old lake cottages built around Lake Geneva in the last century. It was designed for comfortable summertime living by the residents and their extended family during 'surge visits.' It includes a family home with sleeping for 20+, a boathouse, stone bridge to ford a stream and a detached garage."

Interior Designer – "The client's motto '*Camp Lake Geneva*' directed all the interior design decisions. This slogan was even inlaid into the walnut bar top.

DESCRIPTION / RESOURCES		
BUILT	2011	
TOTAL AREA	12,000+ SF on 3 Levels	
STYLE	Shingle Style Estate	
HOME DESIGN	McCormack + Etten / Architects - Lake Geneva, WI	
INTERIOR DESIGN	Page One Interiors - Adele Lampert, ASID - Barrington, IL	
LANDSCAPE DESIGN	Rocco Fiore & Sons - Libertyville, IL	
G.C.	Scherrer Construction Co., Inc. - Jim Scherrer - Burlington, WI	
WINDOWS	Lake Geneva Window & Door - Williams Bay, WI - Marvin	
KITCHEN	Lange Custom Woodworking - Lake Geneva, WI	
AUTOMATION	Techteriors, Inc. - Mequon, WI	
DOCKS	Pier Docktors - Fontana, WI	
PHOTOGRAPHY	Bruce Thompson - Paul Schlissman & Ron McCormack	

The design goal was to create a warm, casual space for a couple to enjoy alone as well as entertain their large family and friends. Bead board, tongue and groove board, and hand scraped, hickory, wide plank floors were used on walls and floors to evoke the typical lake cottages feel.

We were part of the team from conception, and were able to attend to all the details: tile layouts, cabinet designs, furnishing and even framing and hanging hundreds of wonderful family photos."

© Thompson

© Schlissman

The GC – "Working with a long, narrow lot complete with a running creek, a stone bridge was constructed to enable access to the construction site. The main home boasts hickory hardwood floors throughout with extensive custom cabinetry and millwork in every room. The dining room and master bedroom include custom curved glass windows to compliment the copper bell roof.

"Geothermal heating and cooling systems include a driveway melt system under brick paving."

DISTINCTIVE HOME XXIII
"Deepwood"

The Owners – "All of our restorations were done with the integrity of the original 1912 design in mind. A Labor Day to Memorial Day renovation – everything except the home's core (living, dining and foyer) was rebuilt, meticulously preserving original woodwork. And the coach house is the original."

The Architect – "Originally designed by a student of Frank Lloyd Wright, this distinctively Prairie Style home suffered from leaks, settling, outdated mechanicals, and low headroom in the lower level. Three-fourths of the home had to be demolished and re-built completely, all done to match the original style, details and finishes."

G.C. – "Our biggest challenge was maintaining the stability of the home while lowering the lower level floor by three feet."

DESCRIPTION / RESOURCES		
BUILT	1912; Remodel: 2001	
TOTAL AREA	7,000 SF on 3 Levels	
STYLE	Prairie Style	
ARCHITECTS	2001 McCormack + Etten / Architects - Lake Geneva, WI - 1912 the late Robert Closson Spencer, Jr.	
INTERIOR DESIGN	Susan Cellmer	
G.C.	Scherrer Construction Co. - Burlington, WI - Jim Scherrer	
DOCKS	Pier Docktors - Fontana, WI	
PHOTOGRAPHY	Glenn Hettinger, AIA	

above: A gas, 4-oven, AGA cooker with warming oven.

"One side of the home was built into land and the other side was literally standing on stilts while the heavy equipment was brought in to do the digging, removal, and pouring of the new lower level. Complimentary features built into this home include a wine cellar, greenhouse, screened porch, in-floor heat, stone veneer accents and copper clad skylights. And all in nine months!"

"It is tempting to attribute the success of the Greek Revival style in the United States to our national identification with Greece as the birthplace of democracy. The Greek Revival home also represented a period of unprecedented prosperity."

DISTINCTIVE HOME XXIV

"The Pillars"

THE COX FAMILY HOME

The Owners – "Our view is spectacular; probably one of the best on the lake. The location in the Glenwood Springs Club makes it only a short walk to the Fontana restaurants, shops and beach. Our home is a great place for family and friends to come together and enjoy the lake activities. Fourth of July is especially notable as we watch the Fontana fireworks from our front stairs. While the summers are amazing, winter offers beautiful scenery and a 'skybox' view of the ice boat races."

The Author – "The home is called 'The Pillars' because the four white Ionic columns are so clearly seen from a large part of the lake. This was an ambitious Greek exercise by the architect using an Ionic temple front."

DESCRIPTION		
BUILT	1890 - Remodeled c2000
TOTAL AREA	7,000 SF on 2 Levels
STYLE	Greek Revival
PIERS/DOCKS	Austin Pier Service Inc. - Walworth, WI Darrell Frederick
STRUCTURAL RESTORATION	2012 - Frank Guido - Construction - Burlington, WI
PHOTOGRAPHY	Glenn Hettinger, AIA

DISTINCTIVE HOME XXV

THE SHODEEN HOME

The Owners – "We wanted to have lake views from all of the rooms and terraces when possible. We also wanted easy comfortable traffic flow whether it was just our family or a group of 40 or more."

Interior Design – "Colors in the home were kept very neutral, soft taupe's graduating from room to room into pale gray and accents of slate and of course splashes of bright colors. All wood work was painted white except by the stairway."

left: The totem pole was a gift from our children on our 50th wedding anniversary. All of the carvings are events in our lives.

The G.C. - "The stair design was problematic. There were no supporting beams so steel platforms had to be installed on the 'middle' landings to support them."

DESCRIPTION / RESOURCES	BUILT	2000
	TOTAL AREA	10,000+ SF on 4 Levels
	STYLE	Shingle Style Estate
	ARCHITECT	Orren Pickell Design - Northfield, IL
	INTERIOR DESIGN	Joan Shodeen - Geneva, IL
	G.C.	Shodeen, Inc. - Geneva, IL
	LANDSCAPE DESIGN	Sherri Mizialko - Walworth, WI
	WINDOWS	Kolbe & Kolbe
	DOCKS	Gage Marine Services - Williams Bay, WI
	PHOTOGRAPHY	Glenn Hettinger, AIA

"Also, after choosing the spindles we decided to install them upside down for a unique look. ...The exterior stones were split to show more texture and depth of color rather than the typical rounded stone."

left: "'*Jeeves*' is the butler's name and he is located in the entry to welcome guests to our home — even though he doesn't say much."

left: " '*Jack the Bear*' was named in memory of our friend, Jack Krueger. In life, Jack was a 'teddy bear.' He lived on Geneva Lake, and even now Jack still has a great lake view."

DISTINCTIVE HOME XXVI
"Casa ve Ventanas"
THE CANTALUPO FAMILY HOME

Owners – "This is our special gathering place for the whole family. It is just so comfortable and worry free. Three generations love the great times of being together here."

Designers – "We were looking for a prominent geometric shape that could be seen from a great distance on the lake. So, we borrowed the octagonal shape that is the home's core from a 100-year-old gazebo on the property. The roof that covers the center space spans 48' and has a cupola at the top. The two-story window has mullions on the upper portion but the lower portion has an unobstructed view of the lake."

"The difficult decision was how to furnish the dramatic spaces. You have to be careful in a home like this not to over decorate. Otherwise it would fight the architecture."

DESCRIPTION / RESOURCES		
BUILT	1980 Rebuilt: 1999	
TOTAL AREA	Unlisted SF on 3 Levels	
STYLE	Contemporary Oriental Cottage	
ARCHITECT	Original Bill Bauhs Remodel: Edward Raap Architect - ret.	
INTERIORS	Edward Raap Architect - ret.	
G.C.	O'Neill Builders - Fontana, WI - John O'Neill	
LANDSCAPE	Sheldon Landscape, Inc. - Lake Geneva, WI - Don Sheldon	
DOCKS	Pier Docktors - Fontana, WI	
RECOGNITION	Feature in "At The Lake" mag. Winter 2012 Feature in Chicago Tribune mag. 1990	
DOCKS	Piers Docktors, Fontanta, WI	
PHOTOGRAPHY	Glenn Hettinger, AIA	

The GC – "Following some extensive travel to Asia the home owners requested a Japanese soaking tub. A swivel mirror was added to draw the eye to the lake views. ...Reminiscent of the grandest hotels, the main staircase railing mimics the lighthouse concept throughout the home."

501

DISTINCTIVE HOME XXVII

"Bluebird Day"

The Owners – "On a snowy day several years ago, we met our builder who steered us into our property that was full of potential for the ultimate family compound. A dilapidated boat house, small guest house, and 1960's ranch home occupied the site, but we could see the potential."

Design/ Builder –"We created design and build stages, choosing to redesign and rebuild the boat and guesthouses to create a pattern language which would flow into the future main house. Clean, bright lines replaced the tired, outdated structures and sunlight found new pathways into the new spaces. Two seasons later we embarked on the design and construction of the home.

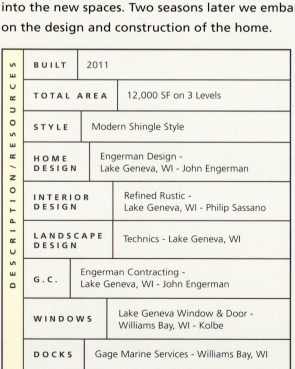

The blue slate roof rises to an open glass cupola over one of the guest bedrooms. Inside, a revolving light beacon spins 360 degrees shedding its light across the shoreline."

DESCRIPTION / RESOURCES		
BUILT	2011	
TOTAL AREA	12,000 SF on 3 Levels	
STYLE	Modern Shingle Style	
HOME DESIGN	Engerman Design - Lake Geneva, WI - John Engerman	
INTERIOR DESIGN	Refined Rustic - Lake Geneva, WI - Philip Sassano	
LANDSCAPE DESIGN	Technics - Lake Geneva, WI	
G.C.	Engerman Contracting - Lake Geneva, WI - John Engerman	
WINDOWS	Lake Geneva Window & Door - Williams Bay, WI - Kolbe	
DOCKS	Gage Marine Services - Williams Bay, WI	
PHOTOGRAPHY	Glenn Hettinger, AIA & John Engerman	

"A custom cinema experience in the motif of a 1930's Zephyr train sits atop the custom garage. The lower level boasts an 'Irish Wharf bar,' which we fabricated utilizing local reclaimed barn wood. We also created a wine room with unique backdrops in the same materials. The home is truly a whimsical delight for all of us that worked on the project."

502A

DISTINCTIVE HOME XXVIII

"Westgate"

The Architect – "Inspired by the historic and elegant coastal homes of New England, this distinctive Shingle Style custom home blends 19th Century charm with modern conveniences. Situated on a bluff, the fashionably highly detailed home creates a unique presence from all vantage points. Finely crafted decorative elements adorn the asymmetrical facades in conjunction with complex fenestration patterns, extensive porches, rusticated facades and a Bronze Clad tower."

"The unique massing lends itself to creating a diverse interior with elaborately appointed rooms."

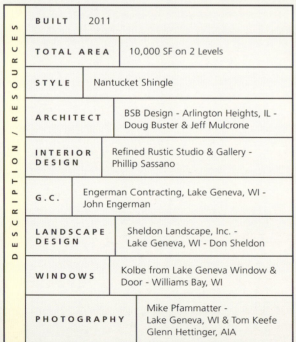

DESCRIPTION / RESOURCES		
BUILT	2011	
TOTAL AREA	10,000 SF on 2 Levels	
STYLE	Nantucket Shingle	
ARCHITECT	BSB Design - Arlington Heights, IL - Doug Buster & Jeff Mulcrone	
INTERIOR DESIGN	Refined Rustic Studio & Gallery - Phillip Sassano	
G.C.	Engerman Contracting, Lake Geneva, WI - John Engerman	
LANDSCAPE DESIGN	Sheldon Landscape, Inc. - Lake Geneva, WI - Don Sheldon	
WINDOWS	Kolbe from Lake Geneva Window & Door - Williams Bay, WI	
PHOTOGRAPHY	Mike Pfammatter - Lake Geneva, WI & Tom Keefe Glenn Hettinger, AIA	

"Our shop fabricated numerous bracketing to blend with properly scaled columns and exterior trim details. If one looks closely, Craftsman nuances exist within multiple shingle applications."

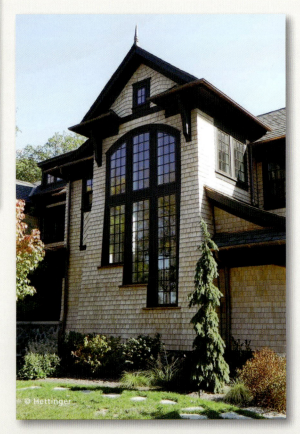

The GC - "In keeping with the convention of the Westgate property, we utilized many of the same elements as the adjoining homes. Configuring the owners' wishes into the 'building box' created a unique and very stylish home."

The Interior Design – "Our interior detailing excels and numerous creative elements were added. One of which was crafting an historic C Scow boat hull into the main entertaining bar."

DISTINCTIVE HOME XXIX

"Westgate"

THE BARTON & JOAN LOVE HOME

Design/ Builder – "In redeveloping the Westgate property, we created three building boxes for homes and deeded the remaining land to the Lake Geneva Conservancy. The current owners wished for a more manageable home and yet wished to reside within this beautiful oak grove overlooking Geneva Lake. We created a common theme for all three homes to borrow from in creating a fine hamlet of homes. All are in good taste and reminiscent of the previous estate.

When dismantling the old structure we took great care in salvaging the hand cut granite stone façade as well as rescuing the oak beams original to the estate. It's unique in its splendor from the old estate and yet is a fully modern and comfortable retreat for its homeowners. The end result is a smaller, brighter version that is a more efficient use of space, energy, and natural resources."

Note that the original and present estate was named in honor of the original owner George Westgate (1917-1940).

DESCRIPTION / RESOURCES		
BUILT	2010	
TOTAL AREA	5,500 SF on 3 Levels	
STYLE	Shingle Style	
DESIGN/ BUILDER	Engerman Design - Lake Geneva, WI - John Engerman	
INTERIOR DESIGN	Barton & Joan Love	
G.C.	Engerman Contracting - Lake Geneva, WI - John Engerman	
KITCHEN	Wisconsin Kitchen Mart - Milwaukee, WI	
LANDSCAPE DESIGN	Fine Gardens	
WINDOWS	Lake Geneva Window & Door - Williams Bay, WI - Kolbe	
PHOTOGRAPHY	Glenn Hettinger, AIA	

DISTINCTIVE HOME XXX

The Owners – "In our search for a contractor we wanted one that had done an equal number of residential and commercial jobs since our new studio had that same mix. Scherrer met that qualification and did an excellent job. Between our friend and architect, Ken Schroeder and Scherrer Construction the whole process was enjoyable"

The Architect – "This new photo studio was designed to be built and cantilevered over an existing foundation. It is part of an ensemble that includes a public lake walk, an existing boathouse, a natural rock wall that separates the main house from the studio, and a newly planted mesic prairie."

"The studio is conceived as a single simple box volume with a glass bay and a red 'landscape wall' to define the entry. A two-story studio volume with wrap around glass faces the north lake view, and will double as living space for future uses. The glass bay appendage can be opened at the corners to convert to a screen porch in the summer. The steel is set off these corners and exposed throughout the studio."

BUILT	Home: 1977 Studio: 2007	
TOTAL AREA	Home: 4,500 SF on 3 Levels Studio: 2,500 SF on 2 Levels	
STYLE	Contemporary	
ARCHITECTS	Home - Ed Rapp, retired; Studio - SMNG-A Architects Ltd., Chicago, IL - Ken Schroeder, FAIA	
LANDSCAPE DESIGN	Sheldon Landscape, Inc Lake Geneva, WI - Don Sheldon	
G.C.	Scherrer Construction Co., Inc. Jim Scherrer - Burlington, WI	
DOCKS	Gage Marine Services - Williams Bay, WI	
RECOGNITION	Chicago magazine - June 2008	
PHOTOGRAPHY	Glenn Hettinger, AIA	

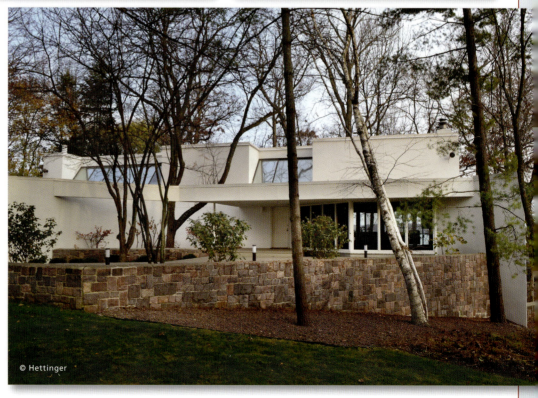

"The box volume is conceived as an industrial container with galvanized cold formed ceiling channels, metal decking, and unstained concrete floor."

"The outside is constructed of a fiber reinforced concrete panel rain screen, accented by a horizontal cedar siding skirt, top and bottom, and a glass and aluminum panel system."

507
DISTINCTIVE HOME XXXI
"Evergreen"

The Architect – "This remodel/addition refined outdoor living to its finest. Creating a transitional exterior space was the key to the transformation of the home. The result was the perfect spot to enjoy the lake under the cover of the shaded porch. For the tranquil evenings, drop the motorized screens to eliminate insects and watch the sunset as the crackling fire takes out the evening chill."

The GC – "We began this project by completing the preliminary drawings from the original designer. In doing so, besides obvious structural analysis, it enabled us to create many of the visual design elements."

DESCRIPTION / RESOURCES		
BUILT	2007; Remodeled: 2011	
TOTAL AREA	11,000 SF on 3 Levels	
STYLE	Shingle Style	
ARCHITECT	2007 Mike Manchester & Engerman Design - Lake Geneva, WI	
ARCHITECT	2011 Jason R. Bernard Architects - Lake Geneva, WI	
G.C.	Engerman Contracting - Lake Geneva, WI - John Engerman	
INTERIOR DESIGN	Page One Interiors - Barrington, IL - Adele Lampert, ASID	
LANDSCAPE DESIGN	Sheldon Landscape, Inc. - Lake Geneva, WI - Don Sheldon	
WINDOWS	Kolbe from Lake Geneva Window & Door - Williams Bay, WI	
DOCKS	Pier Docktors - Fontana, WI	
PHOTOGRAPHY	Matt Mason Photography - Lake Geneva, WI & Paul Schlismann & Glenn Hettinger, AIA	

"Hence, detailing such as the 'Chippendale' style railings, window design, stone masonry and others created a real opportunity to shine."

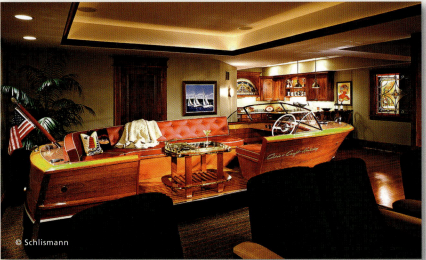

left: "A surprise was the addition of a refurbished boat by Gage Marine in the lower level for media seating. There were nervous moments when a dozen men maneuvered it through the double doors within inches of clearance. It fit! Yeah!"

"Because of the great ideas provided by the interior designer and the client, the interior details are rich and surprising. We even redirected several salvaged antique mantels from a previous lakefront estate and reworked them in our shop to fit the new masonry openings. The entire project really came together in a wonderful way."

510

DISTINCTIVE HOME XXXII

THE MORRIS FAMILY HOME

The Architect – "What to do when your client adds an indoor swimming pool to the program just before going out to bids? We push and shove a bit, get creative, and voila! A 1,400 SF glazed swimming pool room becomes a beautiful transition from the rec room to the lake, complete with a spa-worthy locker room."

DESCRIPTION / RESOURCES		
	BUILT	2000
	TOTAL AREA	9,000 SF on 3 Levels
	STYLE	Contemporary Shingle Cottage
	ARCHITECT	McCormack + Etten / Architects - Lake Geneva, WI
	LANDSCAPE DESIGN	Paul Swartz Nursery & Landscape - Burlington, WI
	WINDOWS	Marvin Windows
	PIERS / DOCKS	Reed's Construction, LLC - Lake Geneva, WI
	PHOTOGRAPHY	Glenn Hettinger, AIA

top: "Our cats remain posed on the stairs, the site for group photos at the end of cherished visits."

left: "The sculpture represents our approach to the lake: fun, friendship, family and never take yourselves too seriously."

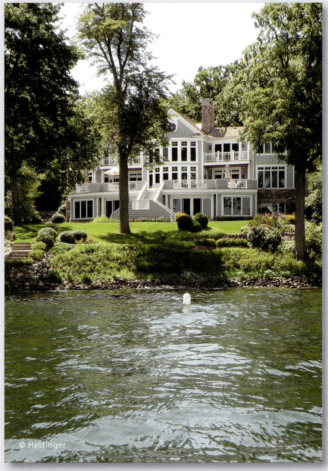

"To maximize spectacular lake views, this home offers three distinctive gabled pods that are skewed 15 degrees apart — a subtle but critical plan twist that is remarkably effective."

The Owners - "We built our home as a gathering spot for friends and family to share great food, endless conversation and all that the lake has to offer."

above: A massive sun deck expands main floor entertaining opportunities from multiple spaces. …And a linear skydome punctuates the deck to spill natural light back into the pool below.

DISTINCTIVE HOME XXXIII
THE R. HAROLD ZOOK
"Clear Sky Lodge"

Clear Sky Lodge has enjoyed iconic status for almost 100 years. This is renowned architect Roscoe Harold Zook's only log hunting lodge. It combines numerous warm welcoming rooms with dramatic spaces and views that incorporate majestic Geneva Lake. At the heart of the home is a 2-story great room that faces the lake.

The Architect – Zook added lots of distinctive and natural elements such as chevron-shaped windows, curving stairways, scalloped wood trim, complex brick and stonework, odd rooflines, uniquely crafted shutters, window boxes, gates and his 'calling card' spider web patterns.

The Logs – The Norway pines used to build this estate were trucked in from Minnesota with 1920 trucks on 1920 roads.

DESCRIPTION/RESOURCES		
BUILT	1918 Remodel: 2006	
TOTAL AREA	14,000 SF on 3 Levels	
STYLE	Eclectic Craftsman Lodge & Adirondack	
ARCHITECT	1937 - the late Roscoe Harold Zook - Hinsdale, IL - 2006 unknown	
INTERIOR DESIGN	Juan Pablo Molyneux	
LANDSCAPE DESIGN	1918: Jen Jensen & Alfred Caldwell 2005: Sheldon Landscape, Inc - Lake Geneva, WI	
KITCHEN	DeGuillo	
LIGHTING	Twilight Solutions - Lake Geneva, WI Jon Adams	
RECOGNITION	National Historic Registry	
DOCKS	Pier Docktors - Fontana, WI	
PHOTOGRAPHY	Matt Mason Photography - Lake Geneva, WI Glenn Hettinger, AIA	

above: The central stairway is a sculptural masterpiece made with uncut, reclaimed and polished wood.

Each log, which ranged between 20" to 30" in diameter and up to 74' in length, was carefully chosen and felled and packed into the bed of the truck to ensure that the wood was not damaged. Norwegian and Swedish craftsman were then brought in to help build the estate.

above: The "lake gazebo," one of the original seven log buildings built on the estate.

South Shore Club Marina
Owners & Guests Only

DISTINCTIVE HOME XXXIV

"Le Manoir"

The South Shore Club was developed as a PUD with 40 lots, 32 of which are in a horseshoe plan that affords lake views to those 32 homes. The architectural restrictions assured that all 40 homes were custom designed and distinctive. The 40 home owners share many amenities including a small marina and a fleet of club boats.

Builder – Custom full masonry fireplaces inside and out, French white oak floors and beams, first and second floor master suites, and stone patios are a few of the items that make this home distinctive.

above: Combining brick and stone work in tasteful masonry detailing.

DESCRIPTION / RESOURCES		
BUILT	2010	
TOTAL AREA	7,400 SF on 3.5 Levels	
STYLE	English Country Revival	
HOME DESIGN	Engerman Design - Lake Geneva, WI - John Engerman	
INTERIOR DESIGN	John & Madeleine Engerman - Lake Geneva, WI	
G.C.	Engerman Contracting - Lake Geneva, WI - John Engerman	
LANDSCAPE DESIGN	Sheldon Landscape, Inc. - Lake Geneva, WI - Don Sheldon	
WINDOWS	Lake Geneva Window & Door Williams Bay, WI - Kolbe Windows	
PHOTOGRAPHY	John Engerman & Glenn Hettinger, AIA	

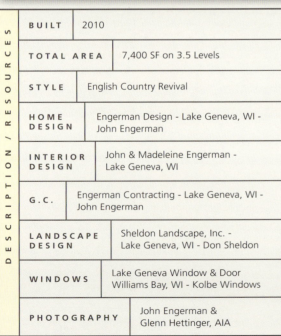
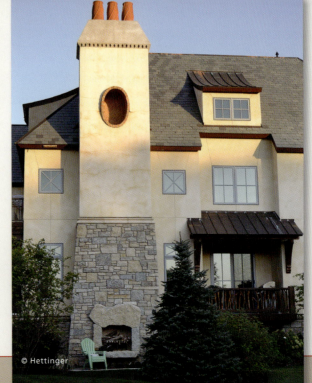

© Hettinger

© Engerman

South Shore Club Marina
Owners & Guests Only

DISTINCTIVE HOME XXXV

"La Maison du Lac"

Design/Builder – "When we designed '*La Maison Du Lac*' our goal was to set it apart from others that share the same architectural guidelines within the community. A careful mix of texture in stone, timber, plaster and slate selections accomplished that goal within our overall design.

Large open spaces as well as multiple bedroom suites provide ample room and fit the recent trend of open space plans. We even designed bedroom suites with shuttered openings looking down into the cathedral great room.

At the exterior we constructed pergola structures of reclaimed cedar timber beams to provide shade from the late afternoon sun and break up the vertical lines."

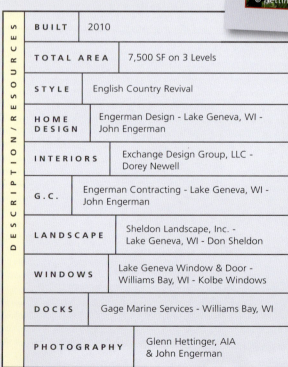

DESCRIPTION / RESOURCES		
BUILT	2010	
TOTAL AREA	7,500 SF on 3 Levels	
STYLE	English Country Revival	
HOME DESIGN	Engerman Design - Lake Geneva, WI - John Engerman	
INTERIORS	Exchange Design Group, LLC - Dorey Newell	
G.C.	Engerman Contracting - Lake Geneva, WI - John Engerman	
LANDSCAPE	Sheldon Landscape, Inc. - Lake Geneva, WI - Don Sheldon	
WINDOWS	Lake Geneva Window & Door - Williams Bay, WI - Kolbe Windows	
DOCKS	Gage Marine Services - Williams Bay, WI	
PHOTOGRAPHY	Glenn Hettinger, AIA & John Engerman	

"Numerous salvaged items were implemented to provide interest and creativity at all three levels. Our stonework took shape from a pile of rubble that at first looked like a bad idea. Masterfully fitted however, the finished work is a real knockout. This project shows that people passionate in their work can really accomplish great things."

South Shore Club Marina
Owners & Guests Only

DISTINCTIVE HOME XXXVI

"Chateau DeVie"

Owners – "We love that the home was designed with lake views from almost every room. We face northwest so we can see the sunsets about 10 months of the year, and we have a great view of Williams Bay and the Beaux art style Yerkes Observatory (built in 1896)."

Interior Designer – "We had the opportunity to design a family home for the generations on beautiful Lake Geneva. Our goal was to select appointments and furnishings to complement the lakeside setting."

"Using color, texture and natural materials, we were able to integrate the indoor and outdoor spaces to create a relaxed but elegant family home."

DESCRIPTION / RESOURCES		
BUILT	2002	
TOTAL AREA	10,000 SF on 3 Levels	
STYLE	French Chateau	
ARCHITECT	Orren Pickell Design Group, LLC - Northfield, IL	
INTERIOR DESIGN	Kathy Stone Interiors, Ltd. - Lake Forest, IL	
G.C.	Orren Pickell Building Group, LLC - Northfield, IL	
LANDSCAPE DESIGN	Mariani Landscape - Lake Bluff, IL - Tony Mariani	
WINDOWS	Estate Windows, Lake Bluff, IL - Hurd & Marvin	
PHOTOGRAPHY	Glenn Hettinger, AIA	

549
DISTINCTIVE HOME XXXVII
"Chateau Du Lac"

Architect – "This home was designed just as the adjacent Military Academy property was being developed into what is now the South Shore Club. Considering the adjacency to the club the owner wanted a home that would look as if it had been there prior to the development, as if this house was once the original house of the entire property. This would create an 'instant history' for a brand new home."

BUILT	2000	
TOTAL AREA	7,500 SF on 2 Levels	
STYLE	French Provincial	
ARCHITECT	Culligan Abraham Architecture - Clarendon Hills, IL	
INTERIOR DESIGN	Refined Rustic Studio & Gallery - Lake Geneva, WI - Phillip Sassano	
G.C.	Visner Builders - Fontana, WI	
WINDOWS	Lake Geneva Window & Door - Williams Bay, WI - Kolbe & Weathersheild	
DOCKS	Austin Pier Service Inc. - Walworth, WI - Darrell Frederick	
PHOTOGRAPHY	Glenn Hettinger, AIA	

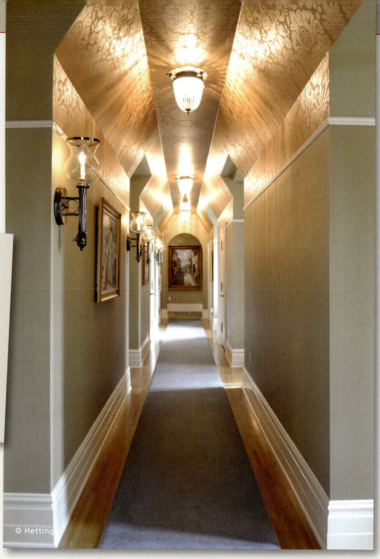

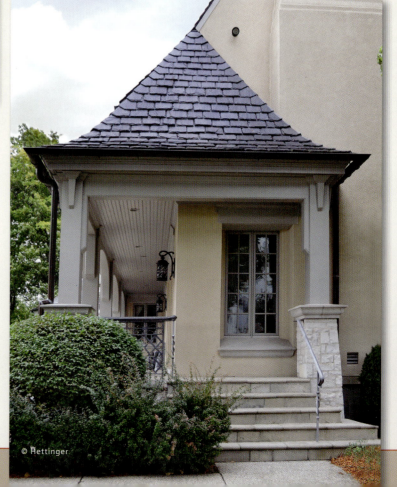

above: As intimate as it is grand, the sophisticated millwork is elegantly scaled for each interior environment.

Architect - "The owner was a designer of many things, clothes, furniture, etc. so the exterior rails and recessed panel where designed more as patterns than typical architectural elements. Thus the basket weave bronze rails across all of the porches and panels below windows."

Interior Designer – "This striking home, boasts both refined and rustic European design elements, that are the hallmark of a relaxed and decidedly upscale lifestyle. Careful attention to detail can be found not only in the interior design, but in the harmonious blend of stone, wood and metal architectural features."

DISTINCTIVE HOME XXXVIII

The Architect – "We don't start out trying to make our designs distinctive. If the project solves the clients' needs and desires first and becomes something nice to look at, that makes it distinctive, but in a subtle way. …All of the homes our clients tended to gravitate towards were farmhouse style homes. We just added a modern twist of more windows and light to it. Any form of good architecture that you see today is a modernized version of something."

"The solution fits the clients' lifestyle today and hopefully for the future, yet the forms are somewhat reminiscent of the past. Lake Geneva has such a wide variety of homes, old and new. We had to be somewhat reverent to that and still make something new."

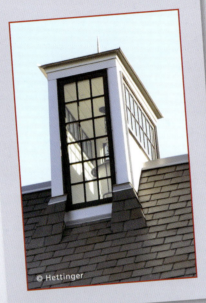

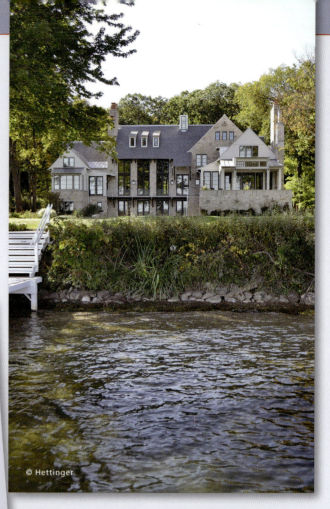

left: A natural light source adjacent to the stairs provides light all the way to the first floor. It can be seen from the exterior on all sides.

above: With enough stone on the home the architect wanted one chimney to feel a little lighter. The metal can be somewhat reflective and therefore blend into the surroundings (trees, sky) and not be too heavy.

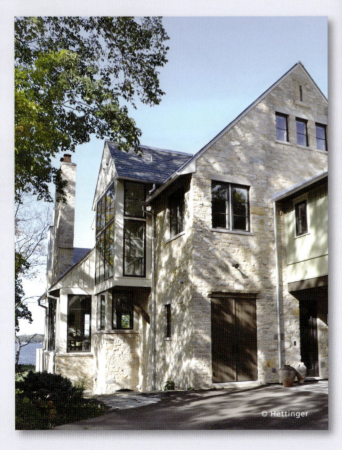

DESCRIPTION / RESOURCES		
BUILT	2011	
TOTAL AREA	Unlisted SF on 3 Levels	
STYLE	Contemporary American Farmhouse	
ARCHITECT	Culligan Abraham Architecture - Clarendon Hills, IL	
LANDSCAPE	Sheldon Landscape, Inc. - Lake Geneva, WI - Don Sheldon	
C. MGR.	Tom Cowan	
WINDOWS	Lake Geneva Window & Door Williams Bay, WI - Kolbe	
DOCKS	Pier Docktors - Fontana, WI	
PHOTOGRAPHY	Michael Abraham & Glenn Hettinger, AIA	

DISTINCTIVE HOME XXXIX
THE BRALEY HOME

The Owners – "Our goal was to build an informal family lake home with room for our children and their families to visit at the same time. We wanted more of a cottage look where the home did not look massive or too big for the lot. We don't have a lot of separate rooms on the main floor. It is more of an open floor plan to get the whole family together. The porch is the most used space for talking, reading, rain watching, cocktails and nighttime fires. We always eat lunch and dinner on the patio while looking at the lake."

Interior Design – "We had collected photos of the things we liked and they were the inspiration for much of what we did. Pictures of boathouses inspired the ceilings, stair newel post, small front hall with a big light fixture, etc. We keep it fairly sparse. Our family comes with all of their stuff, I get fresh flowers and food and then it is full and alive."

DESCRIPTION/RESOURCES		
BUILT	2000	
TOTAL AREA	Unlisted SF on 2 Levels	
STYLE	Lake Shingle Style	
ARCHITECT	McCormack + Etten / Architects - Lake Geneva, WI	
INTERIOR DESIGN	Wynwood Builders Design Team - Algonquin, IL	
LANDSCAPE DESIGN	Wynwood Builders Design Team - Algonquin, IL	
G.C.	Wynwood Builders - H.R. Braley - Algonquin, IL	
WINDOWS	Lake Geneva Window & Door - Williams Bay, WI - Kolbe	
DOCKS	Pier Docktors - Fontana, WI	
PHOTOGRAPHY	Glenn Hettinger, AIA	

Architect – "The best client is an educated one, and there is no residential client more educated than a home builder himself. Thus our design process for this home was mostly one of creating a form and aesthetic for what the owner clearly knew they wanted functionally. The results are stunning - a home well proportioned to the property and perfectly sited to the land and lakeshore. This is an especially inviting and charming home with spectacular lake views from all the primary spaces."

"It has an open, flowing main floor plan that is comfortable for entertaining large groups and yet offers cozy spaces for one or two. The 3-sided screened porch with vaulted ceiling and large stone fireplace is certainly a favorite space for gathering. Extensive exterior terracing extends the interior living space outdoors, over which timber pergolas give partial shade when needed in summer."

DISTINCTIVE HOME XL

"Gudvalsignat Hem"
(Swedish for God's Blessed Home)

THE ANDERSON HOME

The Owners – "The name of our home is meaningful only to our family. It reminds us of our Swedish grandparents and of how blessed we are to live at Lake Geneva. Its casual ambiance is conducive to entertaining and to hosting our many family gatherings. A view from the front door draws you in to enjoy lake views from every room except two."

above: "The Eagle" a Class A scow.

DESCRIPTION / RESOURCES		
BUILT	2001	
TOTAL AREA	10,000 SF on 3 Levels	
STYLE	Lake Shingle Style	
ARCHITECT	Atelier Tilton, LLC - Chicago, IL - John D. Tilton	
INTERIOR DESIGN	W.W. Design - Chicago, IL Arlyn Goodman	
G.C.	Hans Fleissner Builders	
LANDSCAPE DESIGN	Hoichi Kurisu - Portland, Oregon	
WINDOWS	Pella	
DOCKS	Pier Docktors - Fontana, WI	
PHOTOGRAPHY	Glenn Hettinger, AIA	

Interior Designer – "Center stage upon entering the home is a luminous rotunda of stained glass in rich reds, blues and greens that provided an irresistible color scheme. Visible from nearly every window is an abundance of flora, and we captured that motif in a Ralph Lauren flower print on a pair of living room sofas."

"These classic elements were invigorated by my clients' substantial collection of contemporary art. By interspersing their art with a few modern pieces of furniture, we added a fresh and surprising layer to a quintessentially traditional home."

The Architect – "The plan footprint and the massing of elements of this design is a serene blend of pure geometric forms with a restrained use of classic detailing and subtle textures. This created a harmonious home which is at one with the land and the water."

above: How do you use a circular basement under the rotunda entry? Line it with special shelves and make a photo gallery. Every frame is the same size and color, but they are used randomly as horizontal or vertical; all pictures have to have been taken at this lake home.

left: The well-organized and fully stocked 'gift-wrapping room.'

DISTINCTIVE HOME XLI
"Stones Throw"
THE HEINZ FAMILY HOME

The Owners – "I knew when I saw the house one quiet summer evening at sunset that this was the place for my family to lay down roots. My wife and I had always been hopeful to find a multigenerational retreat and this spectacular home and location has lived up to those expectations. Our large family is spread out throughout the United States, but still makes time to return here several times every summer."

BUILT	2001; Remodeled 2011
TOTAL AREA	10,000 SF on 3 Levels
STYLE	Colonial Revival
INTERIOR DESIGN	Bradley Interiors, Ltd. - Evanston, IL - Sheila Bradley
LANDSCAPE DESIGN	Northwinds Perennial Farm - Springfield, WI
SPA	Boilini Company - Libertyville, IL
DOCKS	Jerry's Pier Service - East Troy, WI
PHOTOGRAPHY	Glenn Hettinger, AIA

The Owners – "Our home sits on over 3-acres of the historical and much desired Black Point Peninsula of Geneva Lake. The property faces west and affords spectacular year-round sunsets to be enjoyed by family and guests. There are many viewing locations in and around the home. It is the quintessential family retreat."

DISTINCTIVE HOME XLII

This 'contemporary white jewel' sits on top of a very high bluff and commands long views of Geneva Lake to the west. There are numerous outside and inside vantage points to watch sunsets all year round.

The largest, 2-story living space of this open plan enjoys a large expanse of tinted glass. It provides great views without allowing too much solar heat gain.

The pool is perfect for swimming laps and doubles as a reflecting pool; as seen in the full-page picture to the right. It stretches from under the home to the very edge of the substantial drop off of the site to the lake.

BUILT	2000
TOTAL AREA	Unlisted on 4 Levels
STYLE	Contemporary
ARCHITECT	Ed Raap (retired) - Chicago, IL
G.C.	JaWort-Lowell, Inc. - Lake Geneva, WI - (dissolved)
LANDSCAPE	Sheldon Landscape, Inc. - Lake Geneva, WI - Don Sheldon
DOCKS	Pier Docktors - Fontana, WI - Larry Quist
PHOTOGRAPHY	Matt Mason & Glenn Hettinger, AIA

© Matt Mason

The dining room seats 14 and can be easily expanded to sit even more. And everyone gets a very nice view.

left: The lake path is occasionally manicured with an actual 'boardwalk' like this because the natural terrain on this steeply sloped site would be frequently washed out and impassable.

ON THE NATIONAL REGISTER OF HISTORIC PLACES SINCE 1994

580

DISTINCTIVE HOME XLIII

"Black Point Estate"

History - This historic treasure encapsulates about 125 years of life on Geneva Lake. The 20-room Victorian "cottage" was owned and enjoyed by the Seipp Family for almost 120 years. Owned by the State of Wisconsin it opened as a museum in 2007 and is now operated by the Wisconsin Historical Society.

DESCRIPTION		
BUILT	1888 Updated: 1940s	
TOTAL AREA	Unlisted SF on 3 Levels	
STYLE	Queen-Anne Style	
ARCHITECT	the late Adolph Cudell - Chicago, IL (1850 - 1910)	
INFORMATION	www.blackpointestate.org & www.cruiselakegeneva.com	
DOCKS	Gage Marine Services - Williams Bay, WI	
PHOTOGRAPHY	Glenn Hettinger, AIA	

Interiors – Today, Black Point is considered to have one of the most intact collections of Victorian furniture, rugs, draperies, artwork and household items in the Midwest. The dining room *(pictured above)* still retains hand-painted walls from 1903, a stained glass window, Mettlach steins and seating for forty around an early Arts & Crafts dining table.

The Site – The property covers nearly eight acres and 620 feet of undisturbed Geneva Lake shoreline. Over the decades the Seipps planted a vast array of evergreen trees. And now seventy-four evergreen species are visible on the hillside in front of the estate.

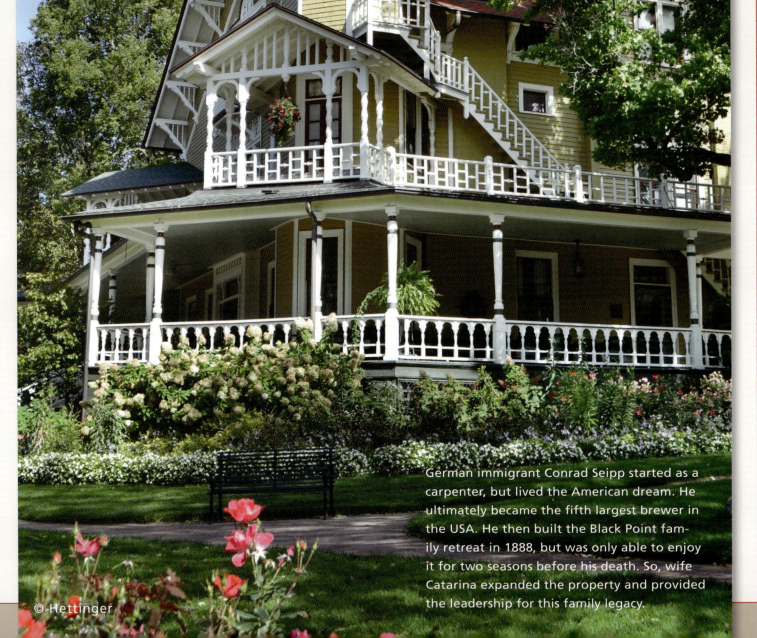

German immigrant Conrad Seipp started as a carpenter, but lived the American dream. He ultimately became the fifth largest brewer in the USA. He then built the Black Point family retreat in 1888, but was only able to enjoy it for two seasons before his death. So, wife Catarina expanded the property and provided the leadership for this family legacy.

696
DISTINCTIVE HOME XLIV
THE LAUGHRIDGE HOME

The Architect – "Inspired by the home featured in the motion picture 'Something's Gotta Give' this unique home features exposed scissor truss beams, varying height bead-board ceilings and a double height family room which lends to its open and airy feeling. This home has 4 bedrooms, 4 bathrooms, a great room and family room as well as a second level sitting area. The exterior of soft cedar shingles brings to mind the Hamptons while complimenting the stone base and chimneys. The home features numerous porches on the first floor; some covered and others terraced which lend to the breathtaking views of Geneva Lake."

BUILT	2006	
TOTAL AREA	5,800 SF on 2 Levels	
STYLE	Cottage Shingle	
ARCHITECT	Myefski Architects, Inc. - Evanston, IL - John Myefski, AIA	
INTERIOR DESIGN	Hickman Design Associates - Chicago, IL Tracy Hickman, ISID	
G.C.	Fischer Fine Home Building, Inc. - Lake Geneva, WI - Tim Fischer	
RECOGNITION	luxe magazine feature - 2006	
PHOTOGRAPHY	Glenn Hettinger, AIA	

DISTINCTIVE HOME LXV

"Welcome Home"

Owners – "We started with two goals for our lake home. We wanted the total environment to be a place where friends and family – today and for future generations – could live comfortably, put up their feet and relax or play hard. There is an emphasis on natural materials – slate, stone, natural beams – that will be low maintenance and virtually indestructible. Where fabrics are used, we not only used durable materials but have warehoused back-ups for it all so, from the youngest to the oldest, all realize this is HOME… enjoy it!"

"We also wanted 'Welcome Home' to be a place that reflected both our love of nature and our intentions to be good stewards of this magnificent site. To showcase the natural setting, rather than center the house on the lawns, and diminish the impact of the nature's bounty, we tucked it into a corner of the 12-acre lot."

above: Another look and feel of the continuous lake path, maintained by the owners.

DESCRIPTION / RESOURCES		
BUILT	2008	
TOTAL AREA	8,500 SF on 2 Levels	
STYLE	Lakefront Manor	
HOME DESIGN	Steve Burnes, Carol Lavin Bernick & John Engermann	
INTERIOR DESIGN	Carol Lavin Bernick	
G.C.	Engerman Contracting, Lake Geneva, WI - John Engerman	
POOL DESIGN	Newmann Pools - Beaver Dam, WI	
LANDSCAPE	Scott Byron & Co., Inc. - Lake Geneva, WI	
DOCKS	Reed's Construction, LLC - Lake Geneva, WI	
PHOTOGRAPHY	Carol Lavin Bernick & Glenn Hettinger, AIA	

"We restored a site in decline and lovingly brought back the land to its original glory. We made the entrance to the home through some of the hundreds of trees which we were able to preserve."

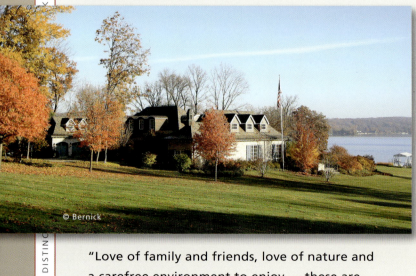

"Love of family and friends, love of nature and a carefree environment to enjoy — these are all the elements that say '*Welcome Home*.'"

"The home's open plan has access to a deck and infinity pool overlooking the lake and the lower level walkout, porches, internal peaks, oversized windows and window seats were all designed to bring nature in."

700B

DISTINCTIVE HOME XLVI

"Windows on Nature"

Owners – "With so many glass walls and corridors, you're inside and outside the home at the same time. The lake is always within sight."

Architect – "The home's unique design, a compound of seven pavilions linked by glassed-in hallways, evolved out of the couple's conversations with me. They looked at plans with barns, silos and other Wisconsin vernacular elements but deemed them too traditional and cut off from nature. Then the couple saw a light-filled house designed by Hugh Newell Jacobsen around the concept of connected pavilions, and inspiration struck. That's when things started to get interesting."

The GC – "In order to create the stunning great room with frameless glass corners, we created a steel exo-skeleton as the frame of the room, much like that of high-rise construction. Then we applied the visible finishes over that frame which allowed the glass to have a floating effect."

DESCRIPTION/RESOURCES		
BUILT	2005	
TOTAL AREA	5,000 SF on 1 Level	
STYLE	Modern Glass Pavilion	
ARCHITECT	von Weise Associates - Chicago, IL Chip von Weise	
INTERIOR DESIGNER	Suzanne Lovell - Chicago & New York	
G.C.	Engerman Contracting - Lake Geneva, WI - John Engerman	
LA & POOL DESIGN	Hoerr Schaudt Landscape Architects Chicago, IL - Douglas Hoerr, FASLA	
PANELIZATION	Sterling Building Systems - Wausau, WI	
RECOGNITION	Veranda Magazine Feature May-June 2011	
STRUCTURE	Thornton Tomasetti Engineers - Chicago & Worldwide	
WINDOWS & GLAZING	Quantum Windows & Doors - Everett, WA	
PHOTOGRAPHY	Glenn Hettinger, AIA	

"Creating a home of glass and contemporary lines requires close attention and a strong skill set amongst all of the tradesmen. Twelve-foot tall spans of glass, exposed plank and timber ceilings, reclaimed floors are just a few of the numerous details creating this distinctive home."

"The bluestone utilized was all cut to close tolerances and carefully laid at all the fireplace and water tables. Building contemporary lines with minimalistic trim requires as much skill and planning as any project with the upmost in detail."

People who live in glass houses either use walled in landscaping or louvers at baths and bedrooms.

DISTINCTIVE HOME XLVII

"Timeless"

THE JOE & JUDY COSENZA HOME

The Owners – "We love having our 7 foot diameter clock and forged bell. As former school teachers we have it ring at 9 am, noon and 3 pm, just like at our school. Our bell is inscribed with 'Bless all those who play here.' It reminds us that we always have the time to give anyone the 'time of day.' "

Architect – "The porches wrap almost all the way around the house allowing guests and residents to experience the woods or the lake depending on which side they are on. Even the interior rooms feel like you are out on the porch. …The face of the clock is mostly transparent, meaning that you can see the hands of the clock from the inside as well and natural light floods into the adjacent rooms of the clock tower."

GC – "The home was designed with careful consideration of the neighbors as well as existing trees, so no trees were removed as the new home nestled right in the footprint of its predecessor. One large challenge was integrating and accepting the 7 foot diameter clock face."

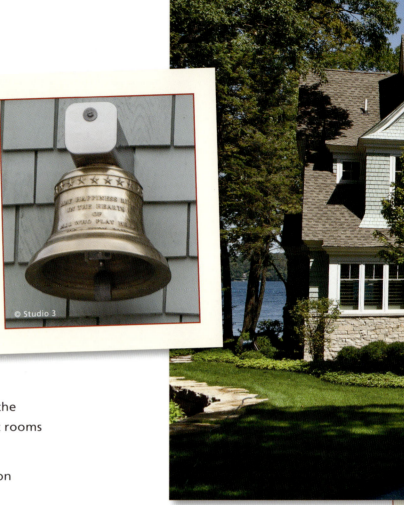

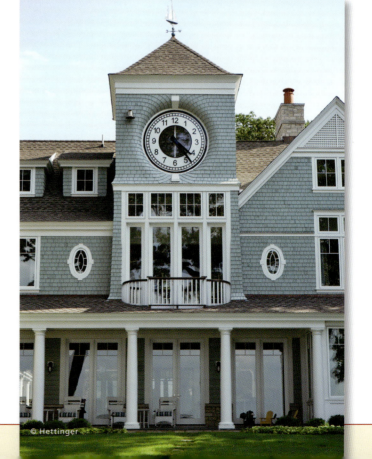

DESCRIPTION / RESOURCES		
BUILT	2011	
TOTAL AREA	8,400 SF on 3 Levels	
STYLE	Nantucket Shingle	
ARCHITECT	Culligan Abraham Architecture - Clarendon Hills, IL - Michael J. Abraham	
INTERIOR DESIGN	Jackie Brigaglio	
G.C.	Engerman Contracting, Inc - Lake Geneva, WI - John Engerman	
PIERS/DOCKS	Jerry's Pier Service - E. Troy, WI	
CLOCK & FORGED BELL	Christoph & Paccard - Charleston, SC - Stan Christoph	
PHOTOGRAPHY	Studio 3 Productions - Ken & Sue Voegele Glenn Hettinger, AIA	

"Exterior flanking shingle sidewalls of the clockface bend and roll inward. Executing this detail, was much like the old days of steaming and bending the cedar shingles as needed in the classic Victorian style. Creating a see-through clock face in this climate also created challenges."

Interior Design – "Our clients wanted their home decorated in light, airy, happy colors and in the Nantucket style. They called it 'refined casual.' We put our heads together with the intention of creating warm and welcoming spaces reminiscent of Nantucket, MA, and that's what resulted."

"Exterior flanking shingle sidewalls of the clockface bend and roll inward. Executing this detail, was much like the old days of steaming and bending the cedar shingles as needed in the classic Victorian style. Creating a see-through clock face in this climate also created challenges."

Interior Design – "Our clients wanted their home decorated in light, airy, happy colors and in the Nantucket style. They called it 'refined casual.' We put our heads together with the intention of creating warm and welcoming spaces reminiscent of Nantucket, MA, and that's what resulted."

PIER 763

DISTINCTIVE HOME XLVIII

"Ashling"

The Owners – "'*Ashling*' means 'Dream or Vision' in Irish and our home has been both the realization of our dreams and the execution of our vision for our growing family. The Lake has this effect on those fortunate enough to live near her. She puts our lives in proper perspective and to have *Ashling* embrace our family as we live by the Lake is the realization of what we thought might be possible."

DESCRIPTION / RESOURCES		
BUILT	2007	
TOTAL AREA	Unlisted SF on 4 Levels	
STYLE	Arts & Crafts	
INTERIOR DESIGNER	Chez Jolie Interiors II - Winnetka, IL Judi Cunningham	
LANDSCAPE DESIGN	Northwind Perennial Farm - Burlington, WI - Roy Diblik	
AUDIO / VIDEO	Premier Systems - Chicago, IL - Ken Johnson	
DOCKS	Reed's Construction, LLC - Lake Geneva, WI	
RECOGNITION	Home Builders' Assoc. of Chicago 2008 - Silver Key (design) & Gold Key (construction) Awards	
PHOTOGRAPHY	Glenn Hettinger, AIA	

"'Ashling' lives well and is very comfortable for us grandparents but the house really comes alive for our three children, their wonderful spouses, and the (currently) five grandchildren, five and younger. The center of activity is the kitchen with its screened porch and fireplace. The little ones love the downstairs game room but there is no place they like better than the lake; either in it or by it."

Interior Designer – "Interior design, at its best, is not about impressing people; it *IS* about inspiring them. The Owners wanted family and friends to feel welcomed, pampered and delighted. Their home is astonishingly beautiful, inside and out, while still feeling deeply comforting. These clients had elegant taste and were knowledgeable with well-defined priorities – all qualities that allow for the interior design process to be both collaborative and exhilarating."

Owner – "It took some years of looking and investigating to find the property on which '*Ashling*' sits. This was a frustrating time but we kept telling ourselves we needed to be patient yet persistent in our search. Now we have two boats. One is named '*Patience*' and the other we call '*Persistence*.'"

774B

DISTINCTIVE HOME XLIX

"Whispering Oaks Lodge"

The Owners – "This home was a labor of love from the moment we bought the lot. We wanted a home that would be open and bright, and packed with every fun thing we could think of, a place our teenage kids would want to bring their friends to, and later their kids. We succeeded in our mission. Our 2 kids, now with their 7 small grandchildren, spend every summer with us. Leaving the home and going back to Florida every fall is a bittersweet time for all of us."

General Contractor – "This home was structurally engineered for tornados. It is a log and cedar home utilizing conventional 2x6 wall framing, as well as 18" diameter spruce logs imported from British Columbia, Canada."

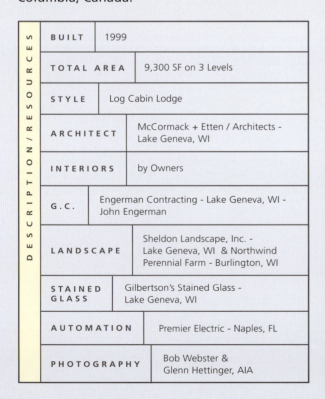

"We used a 5"x7" welded tubular-steel sub-frame, hidden behind all of the vertical half logs, which was all tied together to a 12" I-beam that is lag bolted to the 18" diameter log holding up the roof peak in the great room. And the whole sub-frame is bolted to the concrete foundation. ...The masonry stone was real Montana stream stone trucked in on flatbed from Montana."

BUILT	1999
TOTAL AREA	9,300 SF on 3 Levels
STYLE	Log Cabin Lodge
ARCHITECT	McCormack + Etten / Architects - Lake Geneva, WI
INTERIORS	by Owners
G.C.	Engerman Contracting - Lake Geneva, WI - John Engerman
LANDSCAPE	Sheldon Landscape, Inc. - Lake Geneva, WI & Northwind Perennial Farm - Burlington, WI
STAINED GLASS	Gilbertson's Stained Glass - Lake Geneva, WI
AUTOMATION	Premier Electric - Naples, FL
PHOTOGRAPHY	Bob Webster & Glenn Hettinger, AIA

Architect - "The Clients' vision was to create a unique 'Log Lodge'-style home. We initially investigated building a true log structure but decided it made more sense to use a conventional framing system incorporating heavy log details and trim. The most distinctive feature is the open glass wall on the north side of the house facing the lake that utilized a very creative framing detail to provide the required wind shear resistance while maintaining the magnificent open vistas the Clients desired."

775

DISTINCTIVE HOME L

"Irish Oaks"

THE O'BRIEN HOME

The Architect – "The Owners came to us with an ambitious program to create a distinctive Shingle-Style home on a long narrow lot. The lot dropped off dramatically toward the lake to the north and 12 feet to the west. We maximized the lake views for the major living spaces by designing to the setback line on the east and a stepped retaining wall on the west side. The interior living spaces expand out to a series of terraces that cascade down toward the lake."

DESCRIPTION / RESOURCES		
BUILT	2011	
TOTAL AREA	Unlisted SF on 3 Levels	
STYLE	Shingle Style Estate	
DESIGN/ BUILD MGR.	HVC Construction Consultants - Lake Forest, IL - Hugh V. Connolly	
ARCHITECT	McCormack + Etten / Architects - Lake Geneva, WI	
MILLWORK & PUB	Hugh V. Connolly with Aday & Sons - Elkhorn, WI	
G.C.	Engerman Contracting - Lake Geneva, WI - John Engerman	
LANDSCAPE CONTRACTOR	Stonetree Landscapes, Inc. - Woodstock, IL - Mike McNulty	
WINDOWS	Lake Geneva Window & Door Williams Bay, WI - Kolbe Windows	
PHOTOGRAPHY	Glenn Hettinger, AIA & John Engerman	

above: Life-like 'Harold' the butler is a good greeter, but not much of a server – actually he doesn't even move.

above: The home incorporates a number of features reflecting the Owners' heritage including a Golden Shamrock at the bottom of the pool and an authentic Irish pub with custom coolers large enough to tap Guinness Stout.

GC – "Building the O'Brien home would be better described as building the O'Brien Estate. A wonderful tennis court and pavilion structure greets the visitor on approach to the main home. The main home overlooks a gunite pool and infinity edge waterfall."

above: This door is one of many Hugh Connolly design ideas; it is the most convenient way to access the master suite, but it's in the foyer and disguised when the Owners want it to 'not be there.'

776

DISTINCTIVE HOME LI

THE MILLER FAMILY HOME

The Owners – "When we began our Lake Geneva family home, we had three goals in mind. One, design a home that is always welcoming, comfortable and fun for family and friends. Two, aim for every room to have a view of beautiful Geneva Lake. Three, reflect our love of the outdoors, embracing the natural setting and allowing us to be thoughtful stewards of our magnificent site. … We love the views, the integration between the indoors and outdoors, and the spectacular sunsets. What a wonderful gathering spot our home has become for family and friends."

© Hettinger

© Hettinger

© Engerman

© Engerman

DESCRIPTION/RESOURCES		
BUILT	2010	
TOTAL AREA	11,000 SF on 3 Levels	
STYLE	Shingle Style Estate	
ARCHITECT	Wade Weissmann Architecture, Inc. - Brown Deer, WI	
INTERIORS	Susan Kroeger, Ltd. - Winnetka, IL	
G.C.	Engerman Contracting - Lake Geneva, WI - John Engerman	
LANDSCAPE	Scott Byron & Co., Inc. - Lake Geneva, WI	
WINDOWS	Lake Geneva Window & Door - Williams Bay, WI - Marvin Windows	
DOCKS	Gage Marine Services - Williams Bay, WI	
AUTOMATION	Avlet, Inc. - Wheaton, IL	
PHOTOGRAPHY	Engerman & Glenn Hettinger, AIA	

The Builder – "The new Home's footprint placed itself within an environmentally sensitive location. After following a rather stringent set of government rules and regulations, we set out to build the home perched above with commanding views. We used extreme care to assure no disturbance to the wetlands between the house and the lake. In creating a 'nestled' look, it required moving massive amounts of earth back against the foundations to create the low profile appearance. …Our roof is covered in a standing seam metal, with well proportioned, exposed rafter tails to further embellish a warm and friendly exterior."

855

DISTINCTIVE HOME LII

"Greenridge"

The Architect – "The 'wow' factor of seeing the lake is usually the main goal for these homes. Given that the main floor of the house is no wider than 35', getting a direct view of the lake through the great room was difficult. But we did it with a 'window wonderland.' The multitude of windows and period details give this home its quintessential cottage look, but it also has all of the elements of the shingle style including the rustic stonework foundations."

The GC – "We had to comply with 30' side-yard setbacks on a 95' wide site. So, we had to build up rather than out and that resulted in 4-stories. Construction over a winter which saw 30-below wind chills was one reason why we used a pre-fabricated panelized system. The framing would have taken us 3 months but instead it only took us 3.5 weeks."

DESCRIPTION/RESOURCES		
BUILT	2003	
TOTAL AREA	4,800 SF on 4 Levels	
STYLE	Shingle Style Cottage	
ARCHITECT	McCormack + Etten / Architects, LLP Lake Geneva, WI - PM Jason Bernard	
INTERIOR DESIGNER	Paper Dolls Furnishings & Jeff Rutter Idea, Inc.	
G.C.	Engerman Contracting - Lake Geneva, WI - John Engerman	
WINDOWS	Vetter Windows & Doors (Now Peachtree)	
PANELIZATION	Sterling Building Systems - Wausau, WI	
RECOGNITION	2003 Vetter Inspired Project Awards Best of Show & featured in NAHB's *Builder Magazine*	
PHOTOGRAPHY	John Engerman & Glenn Hettinger, AIA	

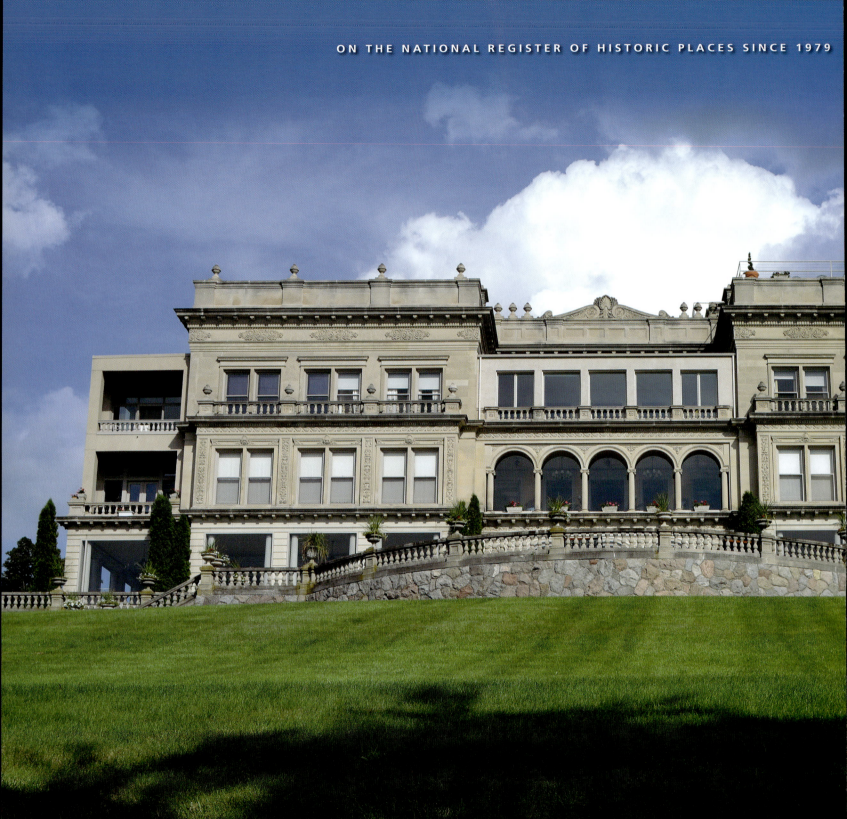

ON THE NATIONAL REGISTER OF HISTORIC PLACES SINCE 1979

880

DISTINCTIVE HOME LIII
"Stone Manor"

The largest and most recognizable estate on Lake Geneva occupies 8 acres. This palatial monolith, originally named '*Younglands*,' was completed in 1901. It included 9 immense bedroom suites on the second floor and another 14 bedrooms on the third floor. In 1938, the Youngs gave the estate to the Order of St. Anne for use as an Episcopal girls' school. In 1945 a new owner renamed it '*Stone Manor*.' It has been a restaurant and apartments and other uses, but eventually it was divided into the present luxury condominiums with an 18-car underground garage. It is listed on the National Register of Historic Places.

DESCRIPTION		
BUILT	1901 by Otto Young
TOTAL AREA	50,000 SF on 5 Levels
STYLE	Italian Renaissance
ARCHITECT	the late Henry Lord Gay, FAIA - (1834 –1921) Chicago, IL
INTERIORS	Lavish hand-carved plaster, rare woods, tapestries and murals.
WALLS	Dressed Bedford Limestone - exterior Tennessee Marble - interior
PHOTOGRAPHY	Matt Mason Photography & Glenn Hettinger, AIA

DISTINCTIVE HOME LIV

"Expect a Miracle"

THE GABLE FAMILY HOME

The Owner – "I used to think the people on the hill were different, but they aren't that different. We all have the same heart that pumps, the same emotions, feelings and desires. There is only one real difference ...the motivation to overcome obstacles!"

Carolyn's foundation, Expect A Miracle, provides relief from some of the daily challenges, allowing mothers to shift more of their energy towards the miracles in their own lives. Please see www.CarolynGable.com.

BUILT	Original 1997; Remodeled: 2000	
TOTAL AREA	15,000 SF on 3 Levels	
STYLE	Georgian Revival	
ARCHITECT	McCormack + Etten / Architects, LLP Lake Geneva, WI	
LANDSCAPE DESIGN	Bertog Landscape Co. - Wheeling, IL	
G.C.	Lowell Management Services, Inc - Lake Geneva, WI - Scott Lowell	
POOL	Barrington Pools, Inc. - South Barrington, IL - Michael Murillo	
DOCKS	Pier Docktors - Fontana, WI	
PHOTOGRAPHY	Glenn Hettinger, AIA	

Architects – "Despite being one of the larger homes on Lake Geneva, this home was originally a large stucco-clad box with little character. We were challenged to give it a major face-lift, and the results brought about a dramatic change. Large gabled porticos were added to the entry and lake facades. The entire home was clad in Hardi-plank, low-maintenance siding and trim, and heavy ornamental trim, columns, and railings were added. A new pool, terrace and stair were built, and a large sun deck and bridge were built on top of the old pool house."

the lake path: Perhaps no homeowner has enhanced their part of the 21-mile lake path more than the author/ speaker/ life coach Carolyn J. Gable. There is much to see and read in front of her home.

887

DISTINCTIVE HOME LV

"Oak Lodge"

The Owners – "We wanted a family friendly, relaxed, lake home feel for a large family but we wanted to keep the historic detail and feel of the home that was originally on the property. We accomplished our goals while creating a very functional home that fits so nicely on the site."

The Architects – "The site was the former Morton Salt Family Estate 'Oak Lodge.' The white wood clapboard sided home presents a majestic facade to the lake. The 'T' shaped home provides an embracing and welcoming form on the driveway approach by the wings of the home extending from the centrally positioned entry."

BUILT	Original: 1883 — New Home: 2009
TOTAL AREA	13,000 SF on 3 Levels
STYLE	Neoclassical
ARCHITECT	Archimage Architects, Ltd. - Chicago, IL - Kirk & Sheryl Stevens
INTERIOR ARCHITECT	Archimage Architects, Ltd. - Chicago, IL
INTERIOR DESIGN	Susan Kroeger, Ltd. - Winnetka, IL
CABINETRY	Lambright Woodworking
LANDSCAPE ARCHITECT/ CONTRACTOR	Chalet Landscape Co. Wilmette, IL - Mike Blackwell Team
G.C.	Scherrer Construction Co., Inc. - Burlington, WI - Jim Scherrer
STRUCTURAL ENGINEER	Kapur & Assoc. - Burlington, WI - Mohammed Zagloul
POOL	Barrington Pools, Inc. - S. Barrington, IL
WINDOWS	Marvin Windows - Burlington Lumber Co.
AUTOMATION	ABT Electronics - Glenview, IL
PHOTOGRAPHY	Glenn Hettinger, AIA

"The lineal section of the home that fronts the lake contains the main living spaces while the wing that extends toward the street has garage spaces and two second floor bedrooms. Strong axial relationships and vertical spaces highlight a dynamic progression of spaces."

Interior Architect – "The home has an additive hierarchical trim system based on room formality, so that there is a consistency throughout the residence. The trim system was integrated into the cabinetry which the architects designed for the entire home."

Interior Designer – "Our goal was to provide furnishings and a color palate which complemented the timeless style of the home while providing a relaxed but elegant consistency throughout the home. The varying saturation of blue hues help to define rooms and reflect the deep blue of the lake."

DISTINCTIVE HOME LVI
"Arrowhead"

The Owners – "We visited the Hanna house in Palo Alto. This crystallized our goal to build an organically designed home based on the principles we saw in there, including the triangular geometry. Our architect successfully captured the essence of Frank Lloyd Wright's 'Hanna House' that we desired. Ken also optimized our lake views from almost everywhere in the house."

The Architect – "The greatest gift an architect can receive from a client is trust. I was fortunate enough to quickly earn the trust of the sophisticated owners, each of whom has an unusually high level of architectural knowledge. The collaboration was always interesting, challenging, and supportive and the finished project is one of which we are all proud. The directive to use the triangular planning grid was taken seriously as practically no walls in the house are at 90 degree angles."

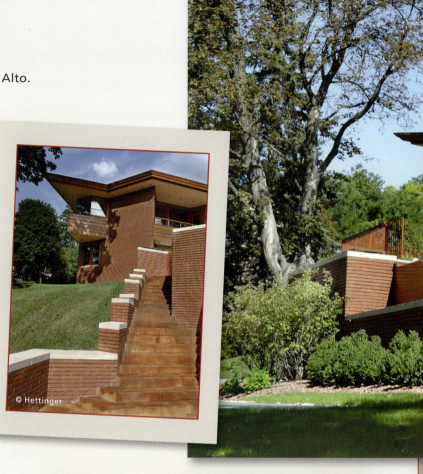

© Hettinger

BUILT	2007 Pool Addition: 2011
TOTAL AREA	5,900 SF on 2 Levels
STYLE	Wrightian Usonian Style
ARCHITECTS	Genesis Architecture - Racine, WI - Ken Dahlin
INTERIOR DESIGN	Amy Carman Design - Milwaukee, WI
G.C.	J.R. Ernest Construction - Vernon Hills, IL - John Ernest
POOL DESIGN	Genesis Architecture - Racine, WI
POOL CONSTRUCTION	Barrington Pools - Barrington, IL
WINDOWS	Eagle Windows
RECOGNITION	Milwaukee Home mag - Mar 2010 Lake & Country mag - Winter 2008
PHOTOGRAPHY	Ken Dahlin & Glenn Hettinger, AIA

© Dahlin

The Builder – "An earthy red brick was used, Norman sized for its horizontal aspect. These were custom made with 60° and 90° angles to work with the plan to eliminate the need for the saw-tooth corner problem caused by unusual angles. Further, the mortar was tinted and horizontal joints were recessed while vertical joints held tight and flush to emphasize the horizontal line."

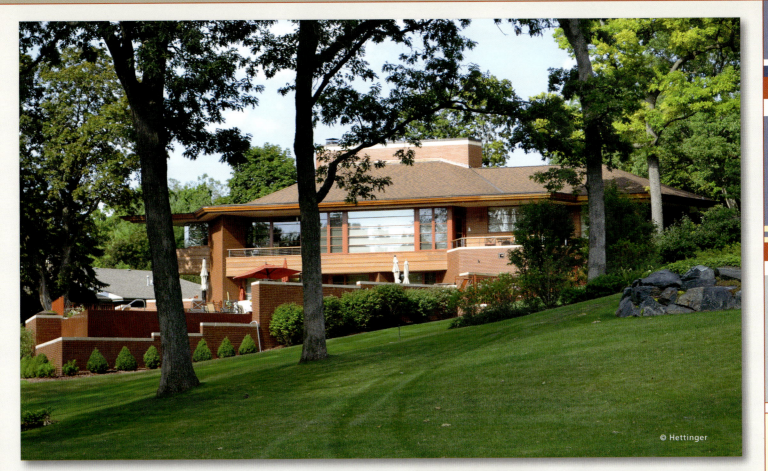

DOWNTOWN
Lake Geneva

Recognized as one of a "Dozen Distinctive Destinations" by the National Trust for Historic Preservation in 2009, Lake Geneva has become a premier destination in Wisconsin and the Midwest.

Over the years, Lake Geneva's downtown has experienced a renaissance as residents, retailers, the city and Chamber of Commerce have worked together to establish a collection of thriving downtown businesses while maintaining the city's charming ambience, all against the beautiful backdrop of Geneva Lake.

Offering a "hometown feel" of genuine friendliness, Lake Geneva is that rare place where everyone goes out of their way for residents and visitors alike. From fine dining and casual eateries, micro breweries and a winery, to spas, boutique shops, and art galleries, Lake Geneva offers something for everyone year-round.

A prime example is the Cornerstone Shop & Gallery, at the corner of Broad and Main streets. A former hardware store and Ben Franklin, this revitalized, nearly 10,000-square-foot family-owned store, carries unique home décor and gift items from around the world - including many American-made artisan products such as hand-blown glass, ceramics, jewelry, exotic wood furniture and original art featuring the Lake Geneva area. Established in 1988, the store's talented designers are constantly creating new displays, and the Cornerstone Shop is widely recognized for its merchandise selection, display presentation, and customer satisfaction.

In addition to excellent shopping and dining, abundant recreational activities, entertainment and events consistently draw crowds to this popular town. Relaxing on the beach, boating and lake tours, hiking, top-notch golf, canopy tours, iceboat racing and more set Lake Geneva apart as a year-round destination. Plus there are citywide events like Winterfest, Taste of Lake Geneva, Oktoberfest, and Lake Geneva Women's Weekend. Add in events hosted by local businesses, such as Gage Marine's bridal fair and the Cornerstone Shop's trademark open houses and other key events, and you have something for everyone to enjoy in beautiful, friendly Lake Geneva.

www.CornerstoneShoppe.com

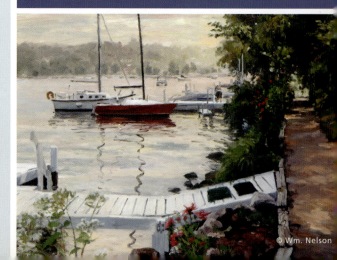

A DISTINCTIVE & VIABLE SMALL DOWNTOWN

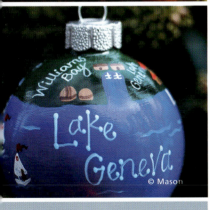

Paintings by:
William Nelson

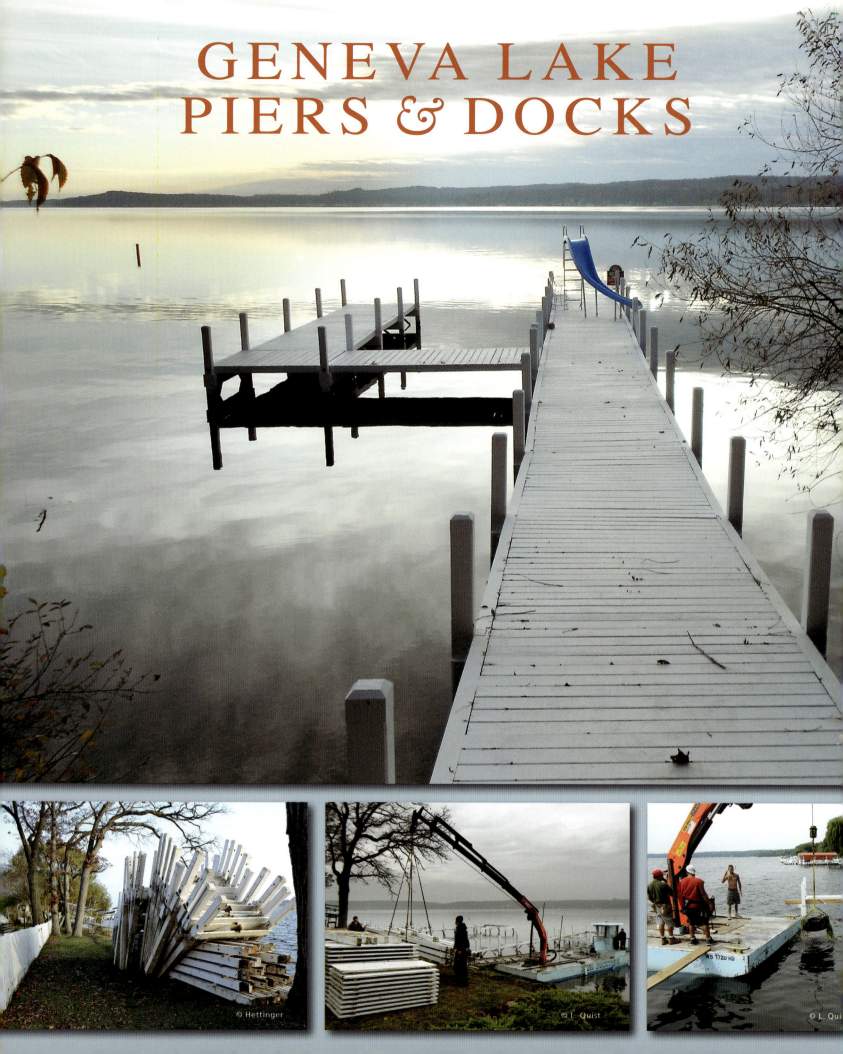

GENEVA LAKE PIERS & DOCKS

THE INS AND OUTS OF
Piers and Docks

Q&A from an interview with Larry Quist, President of Pier Docktors in Fontana, WI – a professional dock company prominent on Lake Geneva since 1979.

www.PierDocktors.com | 262.275.5354

Q1: *Docks, boat canopies and boatlifts in the south stay in the water all year round. So, why do all of the docks in Wisconsin have to be pulled out before winter?*
A1: Most every year Wisconsin lakes freeze and usually freeze thick enough for cars and trucks to drive on it. There are two major ways that this ice would smash a pier if left in over the winter: 1. Ice expansion/ contraction, and 2. Ice flow. When ice thaws in the spring it cracks and flows like a mini glacier – crushing anything in its wake. Any docks left in winter, would be nothing but toothpicks come springtime.

Q2: *When do the docks get removed and then replaced?*
A2: The homeowners try to use their lake homes every weekend of good weather possible. That means no one wants to give up their docks and lake access until at least October. Then they are equally anxious to get back in the water as soon as the ice has thawed in March.

Q3: *Who does the fall removal and then rebuilds in the spring?*
A3: On smaller lakes with smaller docks many owners do this themselves or with the help of their neighbors. But on a big, deep-water lake like Lake Geneva hardly any owners do it themselves. There are about 7 professional companies like mine that have the right equipment and experience that do all of this.

Q4: *Where are the docks stored all winter?*
A4: All of the docks and boatlifts are piled up right on the shore with an attempt not to block the 21-mile footpath around the lake. Area marinas winterize and store the boats.

Q5: *Can the docks be any size and color that the owners want?*
A5: There are zoning laws and codes that dictate the size and location of the docks. Because of 12'-6" side-yard setbacks docks are a minimum of 25' away from their neighbors' dock. The longest the docks can be is 100' extended from the shoreline and the widest the docks can be is 8'. There is no law that says they have to be painted white, but it is the tradition.

DISTINCTIVE ARCHITECTURE

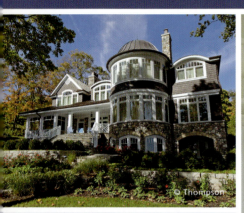

www.McCormackEtten.com

DESIGNING DISTINCTIVE
Lake Homes

Let's get one thing straight. The front of a lake home faces the lake and the back of the home faces the street.

It may be called a cabin, a cottage, or an estate, but it means the same thing to those fortunate enough to own one. A lake home offers shelter and a sense of place near the water's edge, where you can escape from the normal routines of life. It means you can slow your pace, smell the fresh air, feel a summer breeze, dip a toe in the water or take a running dive off the pier.

A good lake home should always maximize views to the water, and secondarily to wooded or landscaped areas. Spaces in the home should be prioritized to align with the user's lifestyle, so that quality time at the lake includes the best views.

Special seasonal spaces like covered porches, screened porches, terraces, sleeping porches, outdoor kitchens, swimming pools, and fire pits all help to maximize "the lake experience."

A great Wisconsin lake home responds to its environment. It offers shade on hot summer days, transitional outdoor spaces in Spring and Fall, and allows the warmth of the sun to penetrate deep into the home during the Winter. Summer at the lake means you rely less on the AC and more on the cooling effects of a lake breeze. Besides, keeping the windows open allows you to hear the waves lapping the shore as you fall asleep.

Most WI lake homes are second homes, and they should be different from your primary home – to remind you that you are indeed in a different and special place. A lake home wants to be more casual than its city counterpart. Materials used at the lake should be softer, earthier, and more natural. It's like wearing sneakers and sandals instead of your weekday wingtips and heels.

An interview with principals Ron McCormack & Ken Etten of McCormack + Etten / Architects – in Lake Geneva, WI since 1973. The wonder and mystique of this beautiful lake have implanted in them a special understanding of "lake home."

LAKE HOME CONSTRUCTION

www.EngermanContracting.com

BUILDING LAKE HOMES
Differently

Everyone wants to move in by Memorial Day for their summer kickoff party!

But building on Geneva Lake has distinctive challenges that need careful consideration. Choose a General Contractor that can give you a realistic project schedule with associated costs.

To move-in Memorial Day most of the construction will happen during the winter months. Construction doesn't stop during the winter, when temperatures can plummet to -20 and snowfalls are measured in feet rather than inches. But it is difficult and you want your GC to have winter construction experience. Fingers, nail guns and hydraulic fluids all might freeze. And heavy machinery is needed to break through 3' of frost to dig foundations.

The topography and environmental impact requirements pose other challenges. Excavating a lake home's foundation is often tricky. Many lake sites have sediment beds which need to be excavated and refilled with solid stone. Still others have natural springs coursing through them which when hit create private lakes and mud beds. Quick thinking and experience can divert disaster.

Indigenous materials and time honored historic building techniques should not be compromised. Granite can be reclaimed from estates that are being renovated and painstakingly refaced for use as building stone. Barn siding, structural beams and plank flooring are salvaged from the barns and outbuildings of statewide farms. Those materials are bleached, whipped and hand scraped with meticulous care before reincarnation.

A lake home should maximize unobstructed lake views. Large individual window units can be arranged to form a "window wall," but specialized construction techniques are needed to address wind resistance, drainage, and weight. The insulation value must also satisfy the state's heat loss and energy regulations.

Many homes require their own deep well for drinking water. Wells can vary in depth from 80 feet to 2,000 feet. Many areas also require their own private septic type systems (POWTS).

Building on Geneva Lake requires a conscientious understanding and a positive working relationship with governmental agencies. Selecting a qualified builder is key to the successful integration of a home with the land, lake and environment.

THIRTY-NINE MORE
HOMES OF DISTINCTION

There are too many distinctive homes from which to choose around Geneva Lake,
in the communities of Williams Bay, Fontana and Lake Geneva.
So, the author thought that you would enjoy a glimpse of at least 39 more distinctive homes.

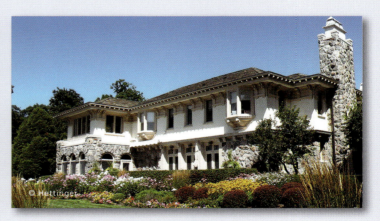

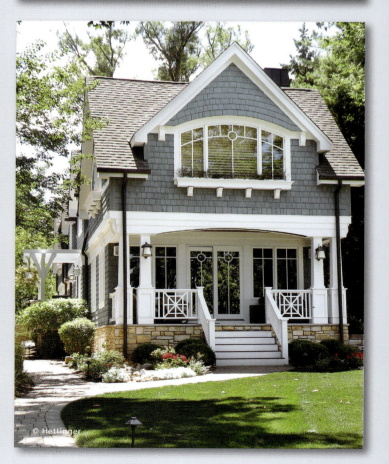

FIFTY-SIX DISTINCTIVE HOMES
DISTINCTIVE GUIDE
Discover more information on these resources by visiting www.DistinctiveHomesOfAmerica.com.

ARCHITECTS & HOME DESIGNERS

Archimage Architects, Ltd.
Chicago, IL
Kirk & Sheryl Stevens
D. Home: P887
www.ArchimageArchitects.com

Architectural Environments
St. Charles, IL
Patrick Marzullo
D. Home: P97

Atelier Tilton LLC
River Forest, IL
John D. Tilton
D. Homes: P163, P558
www.AtelierTilton.com

BSB Design
Arlington Heights, IL
Doug Buster
& Jeff Mulcrone
D. Home: P502A
www.BSBDesign.com

Burns + Beyerl Architects
Chicago, IL
Steve Burns
D. Home: P700A

Cornerstone Designs
Woodinville, WA
Troy Clymer
D. Home: P363

Culligan Abraham Architecture
Clarendon Hills, IL
Michael Abraham
D. Homes: P90, P163A, P549, P553, P763
www.CulliganAbrahamArchitecture.com

Edward Raap Architect
Chicago, IL - retired
D. Homes: P495, P578

Engerman Design
Lake Geneva, WI
John Engerman
D. Homes: P156, P502B, P548-14, P548-36, P700A
www.EngermanContracting.com

Fred Polito Architect
Northbrook, IL
D. Home: P48

GDH Architects, P.A.
Ponte Vedra Beach, FL
Glenn D. Hettinger, AIA, ICAA
D.Homes: Book Author
www.GDHArchitects.com

Genesis Architecture
Racine, WI
Ken Dahlin
D. Home: P888

Hans Fleissner Builders
D. Home: P558

The late Henry Lord Gay, FAIA
Chicago, IL – P880

Jason R. Bernard Architects
Lake Geneva, WI
Jason Bernard
D.Homes: P74, P507, P885
www.LakeGenevaArchitect.com

McCormack + Etten / Architects
Lake Geneva, WI
Ron McCormack
& Ken Etten
D. Homes: P50, P74B, P132A, P166, P183, P233, P378, P394A, P397, P510, P555, P774B, P775, P885, P882
www.McCormackEtten.com

MGLM Architects
Chicago, IL
Peter LoGiudice
D. Home: P21
www.MGLMArchitects.com

Myefski Architects, Inc.
Evanston, IL
John Myefski, AIA
D. Home: P696

Orren Pickell Design
Northfield, IL
D. Home: P493

The late R. Harold Zook
Chicago, IL
D. Homes: P21, P518

R. R. Browne Architects
West Dundee, IL
Rick Browne, RA
D. Home: P101
www.RRBrownArchitects.com

Shepley, Rutan & Coolidge
Boston, MA
D. Home: P62

von Weise Associates
Chicago, IL
Chip von Weise
D. Home: P700B

INTERIOR DESIGN & DECORATING

Amy Carman Design
Milwaukee, WI
D. Home: P888

Atelier Tilton LLC - Chicago, IL
John D. Tilton - D.Home: P163

Aubrey Johnson, Ltd.
Milwaukee, WI
Aubrey Johnson
D. Home: P182
www.AubreyJohnson.com

Carol Lavin Bernick
D. Home: P700A

Chez Jolie Interiors II
Winnetka, IL - Judi Cunningham
D. Home: P770A

Christine Eddins
D. Home: P161

Glen Lusby Interiors
Chicago, IL
Glen Lusby
D. Home: P90
www.GlenLusbyInteriors.com

Ginny Blasco Design Studio, Inc.
Chicago, IL
D. Home: P101

Hickman Design Associates
Chicago, IL
Tracy Hickman, ISID
D. Home: P696

Hugh V. Connolly
Lake Forest, IL
D. Home: P775

Interior Changes
Elkhorn, WI
Beth Welsh
D. Home: P363

Interiors II, Ltd.
Chicago, IL
Barbara Lioni &
James Zidlicky
D. Home: P48

Jackie Brigaglio
D. Home: P763

Joan Shodeen - Geneva, IL
D. Home: P493

Juan Pablo Molyneux
D. Home: P518

Kathy Stone Interiors, Ltd.
Lake Forest, IL
D. Home: P548

MGLM Architects
Chicago, IL
Peter LoGiudice
D.Home: P21

Nannette Farina Interiors
San Diego, CA
Karen Gentile &
Nannette Farina
D. Home: P553

Page One Interiors
Burlington, IL
Adele Lampert
D. Home: P50,
P132A, P394A, P507
InteriorsPageOne.com

Paper Dolls Furnishings &
Jeff Rutter Idea, Inc.
D. Home: P885

Refined Rustic Studio & Gallery
Lake Geneva, WI
Phillip Sassano
D. Home: P501, P502A, P549
info@RefinedRustic.com

Susan Kroeger, Ltd.
Winnetka, IL
D. Homes:
P776, P887
www.SusanKroeger.com

Suzanne Lovell, Inc.
Chicago & New York
D. Home: P700B

W.W. Design
Chicago, IL - Arlyn Goodman
D. Home: P558

Wynwood Builders
Design Team - St. Charles, IL
D. Home: P555

GENERAL CONTRACTORS

Ciciora Custom Builders, LLC
Mgr. John Ciciora – P97

Engerman Contracting
Lake Geneva, WI
John Engerman –
P132A, P156, P501,
P502A, P502B, P507, P548-14,
P548-36, P763, P774B, P775,
P885
www.EngermanContracting.com

Fisher Fine Home Building, Inc.
Lake Geneva, WI
Tim Fischer – P378, P696

Frank Guido Construction
Burlington, WI – P457

HVC Construction Consultants
Lake Forest, IL – P775

Hummel Construction
Delavan, WI
Chris Hummel - P163A

J.R. Ernest Construction
Vernon Hills, IL
John Ernest – P888

JoWort-Lowell Construction
Lake Geneva, WI – P578

Lowell Mgt. Services
Lake Geneva, WI
Scott Lowell –
P21, P363, P882
www.LowellManagement.com

Monstma Builders, Inc.
Delavan, WI
Ted Montsma, retired – P74B

O'Neil Builders, Inc.
Lake Geneva, WI
John O'Neil –
P233, P495

Orren Pickell Building Group, LLC
Northfield, IL
Kevin Batz - P166, P548

Scherrer Construction Co., Inc.
Jim Scherrer –
Burlington, WI –
P48, P50, P90, P182,
P397, P505, P887
www.ScherrerConstruction.com

ShoDeen, Inc.
Geneva, IL – P493

South Shore Custom Homes, Inc.
Fontana, WI
Tony Osnacz – P161

State Construction Company
Niels Andersen – P163

Visner Builders
Fontana, WI – P549

Wynwood Builders
Algonquin, IL
H.R. Braley – P555

LANDSCAPING

Artemisia Landscape Architecture
Chicago, IL - Maria Smithburg
D.Home: P90

Botanica Fine Gardens & Landscapes
Lake Geneva, WI – P97, P101

John M. Staab, Landscape Architect
The Brickman Group, Ltd
Long Grove, IL
D.Homes: P74B
john.staab@brickmangroup.com

ILT Vignocchi Landscape
Waucanda, IL
Aaron Zack, ASLA - P163A
www.iltvignocchi.com

Mariani Landscape
Lake Bluff, IL
John Mariani
D.Homes: P21, P548

Northwind Perennial Farm
Burlington, WI - Roy Diblik
D.Home: P770A

Paul Swartz Nursery & Landscape
Burlington, WI
D.Homes: P182, P183, P233, P378, P510
www.paulswartznursery.com

Rocco Fiore & Sons
Libertyville, IL
D.Home: P394A

Sheldon Landscape, Inc.
Lake Geneva, WI
Don Sheldon
D.Homes: P163, P495, P502A, P502B, P505, P507, P548, P553, P558, P578, P774B
www.SheldonLandscape.com

Stonetree Landscapes, Inc.
Woodstock, IL
Mike McNulty
D.D.Home: P775
www.StonetreeLandscapes.net

Van Zelst, Inc.
T. David Van Zelst, ASLA
Wadsworth, IL
D.Home: P50
www.VanZeist.com

Wynwood Builders Design Team
St. Charles, IL - D.Home: P555

OUTDOOR LIGHTING

Twilight Solutions
Lake Geneva, WI
Jon Adams
D.Homes: P50, P97, P101, P363
www.Twilight-Solutions.com

Jack Gabriel Di Clementi,
Wilmette, IL – D.Home: P90

Estate Lighting, Inc.
Richmond, IL
Tim Tachney
D.Home: P162
www.EstateLighting.net

PIERS & DOCKS

Austin Pier Service Inc.
Walworth, WI
Darrell Frederick
D.Homes: P101, P233, P457, P549
www.AustinPierService.com

Gage Marine
Williams Bay, WI
P50, P161, P182, P183, P493, P501, P505, P548, P580, P776
www.GageMarine.com

Pier Docktors, Inc.
Fontana, WI
Larry Quist
D.Homes: P394A, P397, P495, P502A, P502B, P507, P553, P558, P578, P882
PierDocktors@yahoo.com

Reed's Construction, LLC
Lake Geneva, WI
Jeff Reed
P378, P770A
www.reedsconstructionllc.com

WINDOWS

Burlington Lumber Co.
Marvin Windows
D.Home: P887

Estate Windows
Lake Bluff, IL -
Hurd & Marvin
D.Home: P548

Kolbe Ultra Sterling Series
D.Home: P161

Lake Geneva Window & Door
Williams Bay, WI

Marvin – P50, P182, P233, P394A

Kolbe – P62, P156, P363, P501, P502A, P502B, P507, P548-14, P553, P774B, P775

Weathershield – P549

www.LakeGenevaWindowAndDoor.com

AUTOMATION/ SOUND

ABT Electronics
Glenview, IL – D.Home: P887

Techteriors, LLC
Mequon, WI
John & Alexandra DeToro
D.Home: P394A
www.techteriors.com

Tunnel Vision Technology
Chicago, IL
David Welles, CTS
D.Home: P90
www.Video.Tunnel1.com

Nugget, Inc.
Barrington, IL
D.Home: P97

Premier Systems
Chicago, IL
Ken Johnson
D.Home: P770A

POOLS

Anchor Pool & Spa
Huntley, IL – Larry Hayes
D.Home: P101

Barrington Pools, Inc.
South Barrington, IL
Michael Murillo
P882, P887, P888
www.Barrington-Pools.com

Drew Kunde Designs – P775

Genesis Architecture
Racine, WI – Ken Dahlin
D.Home: P888

Hoerr Schaudt Landscape Architects
Chicago, IL
Douglas Hoerr, FASLA
D.Home: P700B
astrickler@HoerrSchaudt.com

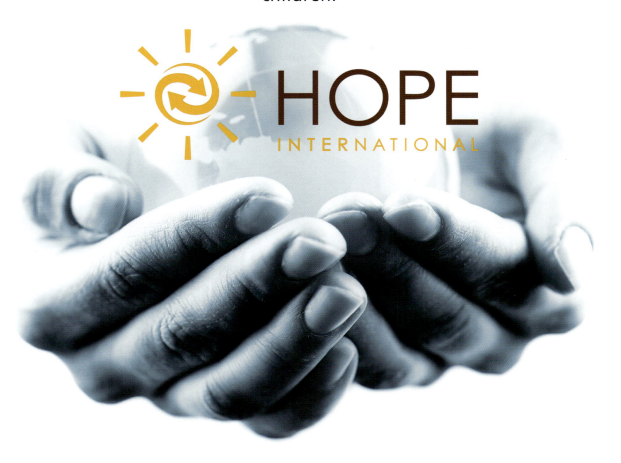

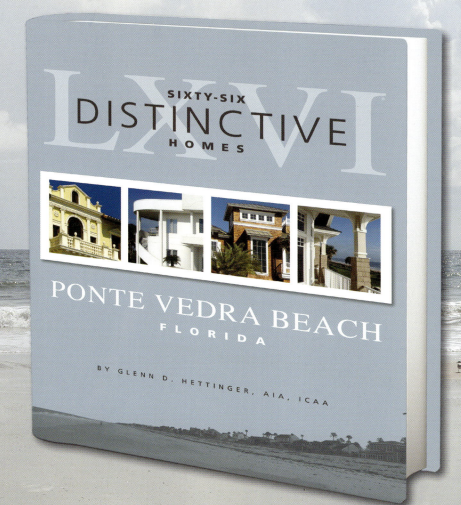

BOOKS
DISTINCTIVE HOMES OF AMERICA

If you wish to order additional copies of *"Distinctive Homes of America"* books please contact us directly.

www.DistinctiveHomesOfAmerica.com
glennhettinger@gmail.com
904.881.8100

ABOUT THE AUTHOR

Glenn D. Hettinger, AIA, ICAA has designed, built and photographed homes for 40 years. As a practicing residential architect and photographer, Glenn recognizes the fine details that make a home distinctive – and is wonderfully adept at capturing them with his lens. Photographing gorgeous homes became his hobby and finally his passion.

He decided to be a 'home architect' in eighth grade. Soon after getting his architecture degree from Iowa State University, he started his own design / build home building company in Madison, WI. He is a principal in GDH Architects, P.A. in Ponte Vedra Beach, FL, where he and his wife raised their four sons.

His first book was '*Sixty-six Distinctive Homes of Ponte Vedra Beach, Florida.*' After its success, Glenn created the '*Distinctive Homes of America*' book series to celebrate and encourage the continuation of American design and craftsmanship of distinctive homes everywhere. His goal is that his books will be a blessing and inspiration to many.